MW01639685

THE BEGGAR II

Crying Out for the Mercy

B.T. Swami

To: a Dear O- In Christ Jesus 12-18-19 From: Pastor Richard

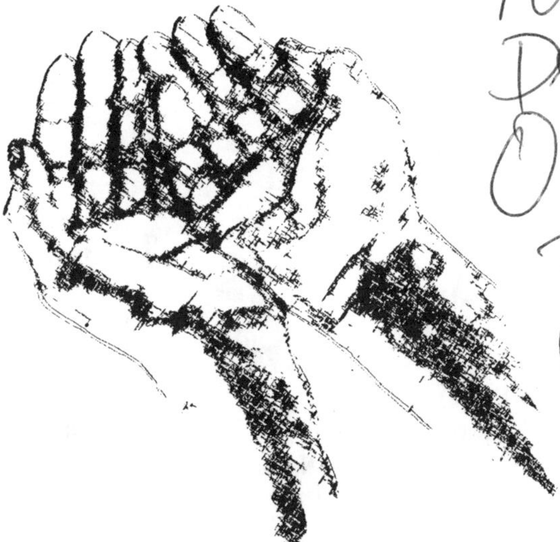

HARI NAMA PRESS

HARI-NAMA PRESS

Copyright © 1998 by John E. Favors

All rights reserved. No part of this book may be reproduced, stored in a retrieval system, or transmitted in any form, by any means, including mechanical, electronic, photocopying, recording, or otherwise, without prior written consent of the publisher.

First printing 1999

Cover and interior design by Stewart Cannon / Logo Loco Graphics
Photography by Adrian R. Reed

Printed in the United States of America

ISBN 1-885414-04-8
Library of Congress card number 98-89613

For more information contact the publisher:
Hari-Nama Press
PO Box 76451
Washington, DC 20013

Dedication

I dedicate this book to all the spiritual mentors who have devoted their lives to serving humanity. May your ever-increasing love, wisdom and strength protect and empower you, that you may continue to pass the Lord's blessings on to your dependents.

Other works by
B.T. Swami
(Swami Krishnapada)

The Beggar
Meditations and Prayers on the Supreme Lord

Spiritual Warrior
Uncovering Spiritual Truths in Psychic Phenomena

Spiritual Warrior II
Transforming Lust into Love

Leadership for an Age of Higher Consciousness
Administration from a Metaphysical Perspective

Contents

Acknowledgments

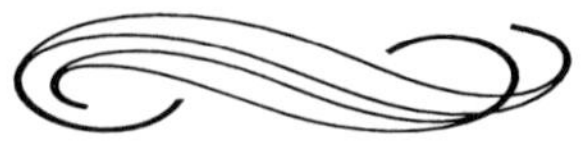

I would like to thank Stewart Cannon for his much appreciated work on the cover, artwork and layout; Adrian R. Reed for his expert photographic work; Marilyn Preston for her many hours of facilitating and assisting in the photo sessions; the many persons who modeled for the artwork; and Makeda Cannon, Joslin Morgan, Marilyn Wood and Adam Kenney for their careful editing of the text.

2 *The Beggar II*

Foreword

What initially attracts most people to a spiritual lifestyle is the prospect of a life filled with peace, harmony and tranquility. Yet we sometimes face more trials and tribulations when taking up a spiritual lifestyle than ever before. As we look at the lives of the great spiritual teachers, we see that they often undergo great challenges and hardships. Even in our own lives, we find that as we endeavor to live a more righteous lifestyle, we often get bombarded with so many temptations, fears and doubts that we may even wonder if being "spiritual" is really worth the effort.

In 1965, Bhakti-Tirtha Swami's spiritual mentor, His Divine Grace A.C. Bhaktivedanta Swami Prabhupada, came to the West to spread the science of *bhakti yoga*, continuous loving service of God. Despite his advanced age and poor health, Srila Prabhupada worked tirelessly to translate the ancient Vedic scriptures and share this advanced knowledge of God consciousness, which had until then been preserved in very closed circles. His superhuman determination and unwavering faith in God and his own spiritual master empowered him to perform the miracles of turning hundreds of otherwise lost, hopeless "hippies" into focused, determined devotees who have now taken up his mission all over the world.

A *guru* or *acharya* is one who leads by his own example. Srila Prabhupada always faced difficulties with an inimitable poise and wisdom that almost magically turned every challenge into an opportunity to glorify the Lord. He never pretended that spiritual life was easy. Rather, he equipped us with tools of love, faith, courage and humility that would enable us to emerge victorious in all our struggles.

I have known Bhakti-Tirtha Swami for many years, and have seen him cling to his firm faith in God and in Srila Prabhupada's teachings to overcome his own obstacles and to help others succeed in their struggles. The meditations in *The Beggar* series begin in states we can easily relate to: depression, fear, loneliness and desperation. These familiar mindsets entrap all of us at one time or another; many remain stagnated in such conditions for years, even lifetimes. As the author shows us, however, challenges can serve as great opportunities for growth. He explains that by reaching out rather than closing ourselves off, and by opening ourselves up to those who have succeeded before us, we too can succeed in helping others.

Bhakti-Tirtha Swami does not portray an overly simplistic path from lost soul to pure devotee. He shows us that at every step new struggles emerge and must be overcome. The route to victory in each case is to make ever stronger connections with the spiritual mentors and guides who, out of compassion and causeless mercy, make themselves available to help us, even though we may stumble and disappoint them many times along the way. The author teaches us how a deep relationship with such advanced souls can pull us through our stagnation and turn our despair into determination.

Bhakti-Tirtha Swami dedicates this book to those who have taken on the role of spiritual mentors in their communities. He tells us that as we explore our own dependence on the guidance, assistance and love of those who have gone before and cared enough to turn back and reach out to us, we should not forget our own responsibility to do the same for those who will come after us. Even though we may not be fully pure, as we progress we may see others fighting battles we have fought, crying out in ways that we ourselves have cried. At these times, Bhakti-Tirtha Swami implores us to remember how important those helping hands have been, and reminds us that we should develop true compassion, integrity and love to share with those under our care.

—Mukunda Goswami

6 *The Beggar II*

Editor's Preface

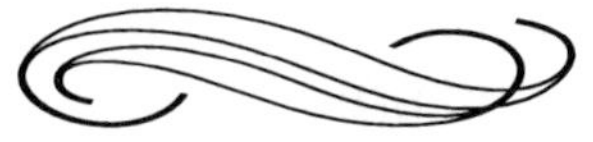

The Beggar series is a collection of meditations and reflections written and shared over the years by His Holiness Bhakti-Tirtha Swami, the world's only African-American *guru* in the Vaishnava tradition. Although new to the Western world, the Vaishnava tradition, brought primarily to the West by His Divine Grace A.C. Bhaktivedanta Swami Prabhupada, has been handed down in an unbroken line from teacher to student for over five thousand years.

One of the principal texts of the Vaishnava tradition is the *Bhagavad-gita*, a transcript of a conversation between the Lord and His devotee, the great general Arjuna. During the course of this conversation, the Lord explains that the ultimate goal of life and the true source of lasting happiness is to be reunited in loving devotional service with Him and His associates. The Lord goes on to explain that, simply out of His love for the living entities He occasionally descends or sends messengers to remind us of our higher calling. Although the names may change—Christ, Allah, Krishna, Buddah, Yahweh—and there may be some external "religious" differences based on time, place and circumstance, the fundamental message is always the same: Continuous loving service to the Lord, often expressed in this lifetime by how we serve and care for each other.

Bhakti-Tirtha Swami makes several references to the *Bhagavad-gita* and other Vedic literatures in the course of these meditations, in some cases speaking to us as if calling out from within the pastimes themselves. While an understanding of Vedic literature does enhance the reading experience, these meditations are definitely not meant exclusively for those in the Vaishnava tradition. Anyone who has ever struggled to persevere on the spiritual path or whose life has been touched by the causeless love and compassion of a genuine spiritual guide will identify with these meditations and find a new appreciation of why and how this guidance has come.

His Holiness addresses the Lord using many different names from the Vedas, to emphasize different moods and relationships between the soul and the Lord—just as the names "Mr. Smith" "Daddy" and "The Boss" may refer to the same person, but illustrate different relationships between the speaker and the subject. We have provided a glossary at the end of the text that includes brief definitions of these names and other terms from the Vedas that may be unfamiliar.

We are very pleased to have the opportunity to share this second set of meditations in *The Beggar* series, and we wish all of our readers a renewed faith in the love and the mercy of the Lord, as they flow to us through the compassionate messengers we know as *guru*.

Author's Notes

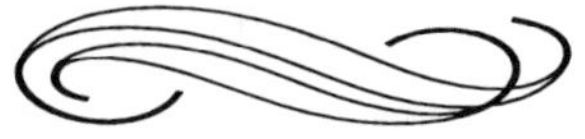

There are ten common types of Vaishnava prayers. These ten forms have been used by many of the great *acharyas*. Srila Narottama Dasa Thakura particularly mentions these in his book titled *Prarthana*, and these same prayers were practically all exhibited in the writings of Srila Bhaktivinoda Thakura. I have written *The Beggar I* and *II* using these ten kinds of prayerful statements, which appear below:

1. **Samprarthanatmika:** Words of direct prayer to the Lord.

2. **Sva-dainya-bodhika:** Words informing the Lord of one's own humility.

3. **Manah-siksa:** Instructions to one's own mind.

4. **Vilapatmika:** Statements of extreme lamentation.

5. **Vaisnava-mahima-prakasika:** Statements revealing the glories of the Lord's devotees.

6. **Sri-guru-vaisnave-vijnapti-rupa:** Supplications made to one's spiritual master, or to the devotees of the Lord.

7. **Sri-dhama-vase-lipsatmika:** Statements revealing the desire to live in the holy places of the Lord's pastimes.

8. **Sadhaka-deher-lalasa-sucika:** Prayers revealing desires to execute regulated devotional service in the body of a practicing devotee.

9. **Siddha-deher-lalasamayi:** Prayers revealing desires to execute spontaneous devotional service in the perfect spiritual body.

10. **Aksepa-bodhika:** Prayers revealing intense grief and sorrow in which one blames oneself for falling into the material world.

THE BEGGAR II

Crying Out for the Mercy

12 The Beggar II

Chapter 1

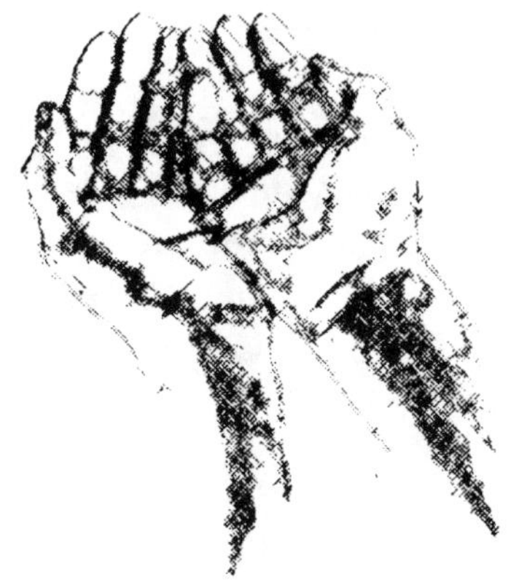

Rescued From Fear

"But you, dear Spirit
Guide, knew just where I
was hiding, and you
sought me out. No one but
a being like you could
have convinced me to
leave my hiding place."

Many years ago, I was in hiding. I was afraid of everyone and everything. All things—animate and inanimate—seemed very threatening to me. I was afraid of the day because it revealed too much pain and activity. But I was even more afraid of the night, because being surrounded by darkness was even more disturbing and depressing.

But you, dear Spirit Guide, knew just where I was hiding, and you sought me out. No one but a being like you could have convinced me to leave my hiding place. No one but you would have had enough interest or compassion to be concerned with a fool as mad as I.

When you came for me and intervened, I was on the verge of committing suicide. The only reason I had delayed so long was because I was afraid it might be painful and I was terrified of what life would be like in a ghost body. If I had known how to eliminate the pain of death and assuredly avoid a ghost body, suicide would have been my immediate solution.

Still, when you first approached me, I did not trust you. I spoke harsh words to you and frequently tried to attack you. But instead of abandoning or destroying me, you simply observed my madness, waiting for the emergence of just an ounce of sanity whose flame could be fanned into normalcy.

Often I seemed to gain some sanity, but soon afterwards I would slide back into darkness. The more you tried to penetrate my consciousness, the more I would close down and fight back. Finally, after many years of your subtle but consistent guidance and tolerance, I gradually began to surrender to your instructions, simply because there was nowhere else to turn.

Once you saw me begin to recover, you momentarily left me on my own. I was still in hiding, still afraid, but also feeling some solace in the thought that you would soon return to help me more. But this time, you didn't return. This time you stayed away.

Suddenly I was in a panic! A silent scream emerged in me: What am I to do now? You rescued me from my hiding place and had begun to make me somewhat sane. Now I have seen too much to go back into full hiding. I've been too informed to remain in such blandness. Still, I am too weak, insecure and immature to venture out alone into a more complete reality. I can only do this with your personal guidance. But you have left me, and what's more, you may never return.

Why did you leave me so early, just as I was shedding my insanity? How could you pull me so far out of my stupor, just to leave me behind? And after speaking such sweet words to me, how can you just leave me in silence? Why would you feed me so fully, only to subject me to a never-ending fast? You've given me far too much to leave me empty-handed. What am I supposed to do now? No one has ever cared for me as you have. No one was ever as concerned as you, and no one can ever replace you.

Every day, I cry my heart out for your association, but where have you gone? Now I'm afraid to leave my hiding place, because I want you to be able to find me whenever—if ever—you should return. I only sleep lightly now, and I even awaken periodically to look about and see if you have come back.

During the day, my eyes rarely rest as I study every movement, shadow and figure, to see if it is yours. I listen attentively to every sound, hoping it will be your voice. Anytime something touches my body, I jump in anticipation, hoping that it is you. And when the air blows a sweet aroma, I suck it into the depths of my being, to see if it resembles your scent.

I have no desire to remain here without your association. Nor do I have any desire or ability to go anywhere without your guidance and companionship. I can neither maintain myself nor destroy myself, move nor be still, without your guidance and association. What do you expect me to do?

Then I heard your soft and soothing voice, full of melody and meaning. It penetrated each cell of my body—piercing every atom. You said: "Beloved, I sought you out because I love you, and because I love you, I stayed for some time to help you sort out the extremity of your mad condition. Now that you are better, I have gone ahead to prepare for your coming, also because I love you. Now, absorb yourself more intensely in everything that I have taught and shared with you, for these were not extraneous lessons. If you continue in this way, you will soon hear, feel and see me again, and we shall be eternally reunited in the service of our beloved Lord.

"Speed up, my dear child, for I am even more anxious for your association than you are for mine. I can't bear to see you suffer. You were not created for suffering. You were created to join us pure ones in the garden of ecstasy, giving pleasure to our eternal Master. So, come soon, beloved; we miss you."

Chapter 2

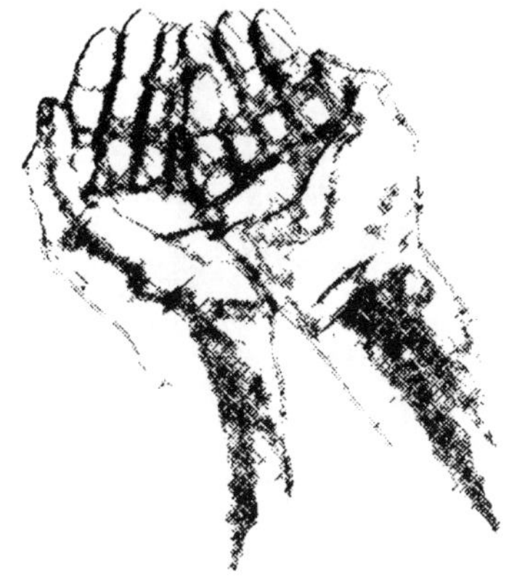

Give Up Your Improper Desires

20 The Beggar II

One day, I found myself in a state of total despair. Gloom, emptiness and depression became familiar pains that ached in each joint of my body. I could not even tell if I was dead or alive. All I knew was that I could distinctly feel gloom and emptiness engulf me in a very hellish environment.

Days, months or perhaps years passed. Who knows, maybe it was decades or centuries? All I know is that when I least expected it, I heard a caring cadence call out to me. I'm not sure whether the voice was singing or speaking. Still, its message was clear and forceful:

"My dear beloved, we have been watching you for many lifetimes, and in each of these lifetimes you have expertly avoided our worshipable Lord and each of His merciful attendants.

"You have poured out your anguish continually, praying silently and aloud. Your tears flowed profusely like a river. We know the extent of your suffering because in your prayers, you described experiences that resembled our own, and because we were once also guilty of similar misconduct. But, beloved, we have come to tell you that you yourself hold the key to unlocking the chambers that will free you from all your imprisoned torment.

"Sometimes you have gone so far as to put the key in the lock. But, my dear, you must now turn the key all the way, push the gigantic gate and walk through."

I pondered this new information. "I have heard such encouraging words before," I thought to myself. "I have always tried hard to do the right thing, but just look at me! I'm still in a pathetic and miserable state." Then, as if aware of everything I thought and experienced, the voice responded with perfect relevance.

"These are not ordinary gates," the voice said. "Understand that it is not enough just to do the right thing. All right things must also be done in the proper consciousness."

Immediately I felt the weight of my deficiencies, and realized how polluted my consciousness had become. The voice continued speaking, giving me a welcome distraction.

"Despite your many deficiencies, I have been drawn to you by the intensity of your greed and desperation for transcendence. In fact, I have been sanctioned by higher authority to reveal your shortcomings to you. I therefore beg you to listen closely, for this is a rare opportunity that may not come again for many lifetimes."

I braced myself for a rude awakening. "I have noticed that you are always vigorously serving your *guru* and the Lord. But this is primarily because you want to be known as a good servant. As far as you're concerned, you have gone everywhere to preach on the Lord's behalf. You have even traveled the world, distributing wonderful books that glorify the Supreme. But in reality, all this was because you yourself wanted to be viewed as a merciful saint.

"It's true that you have also met with the rich and famous, and we see that you have acquired numerous students, using God and *guru* as your bait. But again, this was all done as an act of self-aggrandizement in order to expand your own circle of influence.

"People are impressed that you have built so many temples, and that you have founded so many spiritual communities. But actually all of these activities were just attempts to increase your own empire. In truth, you have not even once honestly served the Supreme; you only used Him and His empowered servants to serve your own idiosyncratic interests.

"How could you believe that the Lord would allow a soft-core criminal like you to enter His abode, simply so you could import your abuse and exploitation to the spiritual kingdom? In everything you do, everything you look at and everything you experience, you are secretly trying to twist the situation into a means for your own enjoyment. But you must give up these improper desires, for until the seeds of these desires are destroyed, they will constantly take root and periodically surface, causing you all sorts of problems and stagnation."

As I listened to this explanation, all the emptiness, gloom, pain and depression I had experienced earlier became incredibly intensified. My first reaction was one of total denial. I wanted to shout out and curse at anything that I could. But instead I channeled that intensity inward and recognized that all of these remarks were unequivocally true.

As soon as I humbly but deeply accepted this full report of my faults, my radical change of consciousness miraculously turned the key. All of a sudden the same voice that had just moments before heavily chastised me addressed me in the gentlest manner. "Now push the gate open with both hands," the voice said.

When I did this, I saw the most beautiful spiritual being, and as soon as he spoke, I realized that he was the one I had been hearing. To my surprise, he warmly embraced me, then pulled me away to look deeply into my eyes. His words cut to the core of me. "My child, it was not really your screaming, your crying or even your change of consciousness that turned the key. It was the prayers of your spiritual master.

"For decades, your spiritual master has been begging, screaming and crying to the Supreme Lord on your behalf—even more loudly and more feelingly than you have cried. Your spiritual master's pitiful begging for your deliverance is what sent me here to free you. You see, you were a beggar who did not know how to beg. But fortunately for you, the cries of your spiritual master pierced the many thick layers of the material universe and summoned my intervention. Ultimately, it was these cries of your spiritual master that actually saved you, for although he is a fully realized soul, his softened heart knows the humble art of begging."

Chapter 3

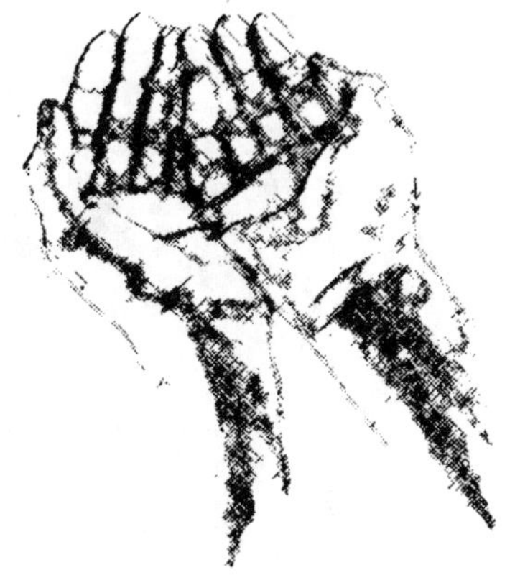

Please Don't Pass Me By

"Just let go of your illusions and release hold of your sinful desires, for as soon as you do this, I will immediately have an escort rush there to bring you back to Me."

Dear Gopinath, Lord of the Gopis, You have promised that as all living entities surrender to You, You will reward them accordingly. You have even said that everyone is on Your path and that for those who surrender to You, You will maintain what they have and supply what they lack. I lack so much and have so little, but I am also on Your path, so perhaps there is some hope for me.

Dear Gopinath, I have so many sinful desires. How will You be able to see me as I walk on Your path? Will not all of my sinful desires obscure Your vision of me? For lifetimes, I have repeatedly been sending many distress calls out into the ether, yet You continue to save others and simply pass me by. Is this because my sinful desires interfere with the distress messages I've been transmitting?

Dear Gopinath, time and again, You rescue Your devotees from all types of demonic threats. Many times, even before the dangers attack, You have already put into motion an arrangement to provide protection. But in my case, You have passed me by, despite the constant attacks I suffer and my numerous pleas for help.

My dearest Gopinath, is there something special You desire of me? You know I have so little to offer; that is why I greatly need You to fulfill Your promise and supply what I lack.

Surely when You promised to supply what each of us lacks, it was before You realized that there would be such needy persons as myself, burdening You with my bereavements.

Dear Gopinath, the many souls You have rescued before me are now in Your association; thus I can no longer be with them or communicate with them as before. I am happy that they are with You, but every time You pass me by, it makes my separation from them even more acute and much more difficult to bear. Maybe You can take pity on me and rescue me next.

Maybe You will even be so kind as to allow me to see Your servants in the spiritual world receiving Your love and protection. Just the vision of their happiness in Your association would be totally satisfying to me. Just hearing a few sweet words of encouragement from Your servants would be the perfection of my ears.

O Lord Gopinath, please perfect my eyes with the vision of one of Your servants attentively tending to Your wishes. Perfect my nose with the scent of a flower tenderly offered to You by one of Your servants.

To taste a morsel of the merciful remnants You have enjoyed from the hands of a personal servant would be the perfection of my tongue, and how I long for such perfection!

If ever I were touched by a servant of Yours who had touched Your glorious Self, I would surely forget that I am a bound prisoner of this material plane, and I would be freed of my material desires.

Dearest Gopinath, how foolish it is for one like myself with so many material desires to long for the touch, sight or sound of one of Your servants. It is even more absurd for one such as me to desire the company of Your Transcendental Lordship. But You Yourself have said that everyone is on Your path, and that You will personally maintain what each of us has, and personally supply what we lack.

Then I heard a tender, even-tempered voice address my concern. The voice said: "Yes, beloved, I will maintain what My devotees have and supply what they lack, for everyone is on My path. But, most importantly, I reward all souls as they surrender. If you fully surrender to Me, not only will you be fully rescued, but You will also realize that I had rescued you even before you emitted your anguished cry and called out for Me to relieve your grief.

"Actually, it is you who have been passing Me by, each and every time I came to receive you. But, you see, I love you so very much that I am prepared to wait for you for millions of lifetimes, even if you overlook Me again and again."

The voice continued: "Just let go of your illusions and release hold of your sinful desires, for as soon as you do this, I will immediately have an escort rush there to bring you back to Me.

"Beloved, at long last, please come home. So many loved ones are ready and waiting to receive you. We are all just waiting for the day when you will stop passing us by! What must we do to make you stop overlooking us?"

Chapter 4

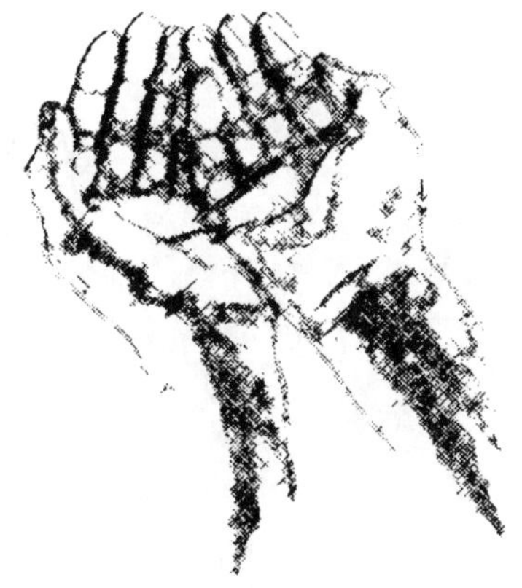

One Should Never See The Lord's Servants As Ordinary

"By My divine arrangement, I allow them constantly to create order out of chaos with their determined poise and detachment."

One Should Never See The Lord's Servants As Ordinary 33

My dear Lord Govinda, sometimes when I reflect on the sages, *acharyas* and saintly personalities, I wonder why we offer such reverence to what sometimes seem to be ordinary persons. Like us, these saints are born, experience sickness, grow old and then die. Most of them meet many challenges throughout their lives. Sometimes they even seem defeated by these challenges.

If these saints are so special and so dear to You, why do so many ordinary events occur in their lives? Why do they meet so many challenges and why do they appear to suffer so intensely?

Lord Govinda chuckled. "Even when I personally descend, I seem to take on the ordinary activities and characteristics of the material environment. However, I have very strongly stated in the *Bhagavad-gita* that only fools believe that I am constrained by ordinary laws and circumstances when I descend. Even My body, though appearing to be human, never has human limitations. But fools never understand My supreme dominion, even when I readily display it.

"The same is true of my pure devotees. When My pure devotees enter these material universes, they powerfully represent Me in so many respects. These devotees make themselves available even to the lowest of demons, just as I do, because their sublime intent is to use every means possible to infiltrate these material insane asylums and release all of the prisoners.

"It is a great offense to think that these devotees are like ordinary inmates of the material world. Not only can such an offense literally stall one's spiritual life, but an individual who thinks this way may even lose the spiritual credits he has attained over lifetimes."

Lord Govinda continued: "Not only are My pure devotees so merciful that they should never be offended, but even the servants of these unalloyed devotees are extremely special. Is it not obvious that those who represent an important project or service are themselves very important also?

"When one offends My pure representative, he is also offending Me! Likewise, when one offends the servants of My representative, this indirect offense to My ambassador is equally offensive to Me. Let us take the converse, for instance. If someone serves and honors My representative, is he not also serving Me?

"If you study this phenomenon closely, you will see why some souls advance rapidly, while others hardly advance at all. In any case, those who think that I, My representatives or their servants are ordinary inmates of these hells are assuredly prolonging their sentences by numerous lifetimes.

"Of course, this is nothing new. When I sent Jesus the Christ of Nazareth to the earth planet, I had him take birth in a barn, and caused him to wander as a scantily clothed itinerant. My representative Prophet Muhammad was totally illiterate. Likewise Lord Buddha, although a prince, could not do any of My work until He became a beggar.

"The same is true of My great devotee Lord Shiva, who lived under a tree. Similarly, although the six *goswamis* of Vrindavan were initially situated in royal professions, in order to serve My mission more fully they had to renounce their luxuries and associate with ruffians. Eventually they, too, had to live under trees.

"When I make My own appearances, I also come alternately as a *brahmana, ksatriya, vaisya* and *sudra.* I sometimes even take on the form of lower animals to increase the chances for liberation of souls in these species, and to increase My own enjoyment. Still, in all cases involving Myself or My pure representatives and their servants, our activities in in this material dungeon are solely for the purpose of rescuing others. To give maximum assistance and guidance to material prisoners, We take on many qualities and activities of this environment. Still, the envious and devious nature of the unfortunate hard-core materialists prevents them from recognizing My greatness or that of My agents. Because they misuse their own abilities and greatness to exploit and manipulate others, they try to trivialize My glorious love, humility, compassion and selfless personalism and that of My helpers. They consider these qualities to be foreign and mundane.

"My great devotee Srila Madhavacarya reiterates this truth in the *Tantra Nirnaya*, saying: 'From Lord Brahma down, all living entities engaged in the service of the Lord are extraordinary.' Madhavacarya knew, as all liberated souls do, that although My devotees may sometimes appear to suffer, this is not actually the case. As My expert servants, the demigods, explain in their prayers to Me, 'Incessant transcendental bliss flows in the minds of those who have even once tasted but a tiny drop ot the nectar from the ocean of My glories. Such exalted devotees forget the tiny reflection of so-called material happiness produced from the material senses of sight and sound. Free from all desires, such devotees are the real friends of all living entities. Offering their minds unto Me and enjoying transcendental bliss, these souls are always expert in achieving the real goal of life...' [*Srimad Bhagavatam* 6.9.39]

"Still, the gross materialist cannot appreciate that I often put My great servants into humble circumstances so that their own beauty and divine power will radiate even more. By My divine arrangement, I allow them constantly to create order out of chaos with their determined poise and detachment. In this way, they help others understand the beauty and power of perseverance and strong faith.

"For this reason, I almost invariably require My pure devotees to struggle against severe and formidable obstacles, so that humankind can see how, despite the greatest of traumas and difficulties, My pure devotees remain loyal to Me and know only Me as their refuge, just as I know only them.

"Just look at My exemplary son, Srila Prabhupada. Did I not start his mission in a most humble and precarious way? I sent Srila Prabhupada out of the holy land of Vrindavan at the advanced age of sixty-nine with only a few dollars in his pocket. His Divine Grace A.C. Bhaktivedanta knew no one in the West, although this part of the world was to become his major field of preaching. Prabhupada wasn't even very expert in the foreign language he had to use in writing his books. In addition, his health was frail. Yet I directed him from within to go to some of the planet's most degraded places and interact with some of society's greatest misfits and upstarts. To show the rare compassion of a pure devotee, I allowed Srila Prabhupada to dwell among many lost souls in order to lead them painstakingly out of their dark existence.

"Thus, anyone who considers Me, My representatives or their servants to be ordinary conditioned souls is condemned to reside in the material spheres of hell for many lifetimes. On the other hand, all those living entities who somehow take full shelter of these secret agents of Mine will surely be rescued in the near future. Similarly, those who serve or assist such agents in their commissions are also up for parole, and should in no way be considered ordinary, insubordinate inmates.

"Yes, when I or My pure representative descends, we certainly appear to be of this world. In fact, to blend in and accomplish our mission, we deliberately appear to eat, sleep, mate and defend just like regular residents of this planet, but nothing could be further from the truth.

"In the same way that demigods from the heavenly planets see the residents of Vrindavan as having four arms like the pure souls in Vaikuntha, from time to time those earthly residents who have eyes to see will get glimpses of My representatives' transcendental forms and attributes. They will be deeply touched and sometimes moved to surrender by such an encounter.

"My dear son," Lord Govinda concluded. "You must become fully selfless and humble, overflowing with compassion and devotion. This will help you fully to appreciate and gaze upon the actual pure form of My extraordinary agents, and will also allow you to become such an agent yourself.

"Beloved, I will continue to come Myself, as I have in the past, and will send many humble and accessible agents. But will you continue to be clouded by lust and greed and thereby deprive yourself of these precious opportunities? Or will you realize that anything connected with Me, My message and My mission is never ordinary or to be taken for granted?

"Please try to recognize the rarity of those individuals known as devotees. Also try to understand that each encounter with one of My agents or his servants should be appreciated and accepted as a most powerful expression of My love!

"Please position yourself better to receive this unconditional love of Mine. It has always been available, but again and again you have deprived yourself of its sweetness by continually doubting and delaying."

Chapter 5

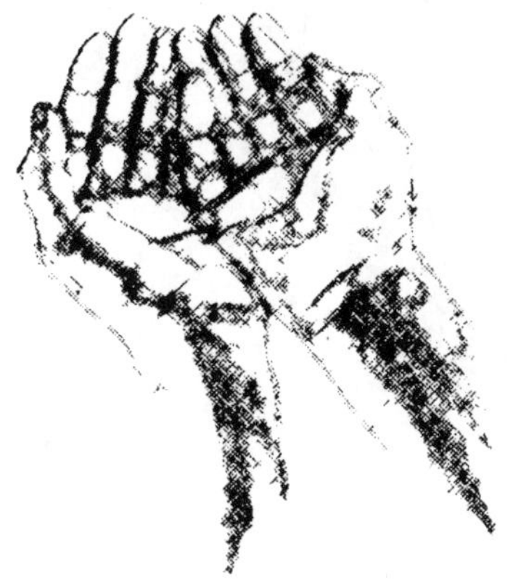

Who But You Could Have Saved Us?

*"When the task
is almost
insurmountable
or seemingly
impossible, an
even more highly
empowered
entity must be
summoned. We
can see that this
is the position of
His Divine
Grace Srila
Prabhupada."*

Who But You Could Have Saved Us?

When there is a very difficult task, a most expert and energetic person must be called in to help the situation. When the task is seemingly impossible, an even more highly empowered entity must be summoned. We can see that this is the position of His Divine Grace Srila Prabhupada, who was summoned into this world to make the impossible become reality.

Dear spiritual master and savior, at the time of your arrival, we were convinced that religious leaders were just politicians and calculating entrepreneurs disguising themselves as good samaritans. Then you came and gave us the rich culture of *bhakti,* which immediately caused us to abandon our nonsensical notions and exchange our destructive attitudes for constructive activity.

Dear spiritual master and savior, at that time, we felt that anyone over thirty was an antiquated dinosaur who could never have anything valuable to offer. Yet, although you were more than twice that age, you brought us the most relevant knowledge in existence, which directly applied to all of our problems.

Dear spiritual master and savior, when you came, we were afraid to be tied down by commitments. We were roaming around with wanderlust, trying to avoid boredom, routine and responsibility. But you not only captured us with your kindness, you then showed us the joy of being responsible, and actually compelled us to commit our lives to your mission.

Dear spiritual master and savior, back in those days, we were convinced that rules and regulations were all relative and useless, until you proved to us that those who refused to embrace rules or regulations were themselves useless and downright menacing to society. Rather than being free, they were the slaves of their sensual impulses.

Dear spiritual master and savior, before you, we had no faith in any authorities. We had lost all respect for organizations and institutions. However, you very intelligently organized us in the spreading of Lord Chaitanya's message, and thus not only showed us the beauty of organization, but allowed us the distinction of introducing the Holy Name to all continents of the planet.

Dear spiritual master and savior, when you first encountered us, our thoughts were crazy, our language was lewd, and almost everything we verbalized was vile and offensive. However, you taught us how to chant the Holy Name, sing sweet *bhajans* and speak Bhagavat philosophy with great fluency and eloquence.

Dear spiritual master and savior, before you, drugs and drinking were our religion, and virtually all of our social contact centered around drug culture. But you miraculously helped us to become free of these addictions and replaced them with genuine ecstasy.

Dear spiritual master and savior, when you first descended, we were behaving like cannibals and eating raw or burnt corpses. We even murdered the children in our women's wombs with great zeal and enthusiasm. Then you mercifully taught us about the soul and how to value all life properly.

Dear spiritual master and savior, all of us were gambling our lives away, pursuing mundane education and speculation and wasting our money through nefarious games of chance. Then your teachings and presence came to help us understand the Absolute Truth and how to share the sacred message of God-consciousness so we could engage in the glorious risk-taking that is authorized by the Lord and His agents.

Dear spiritual master and savior, our most honorable guide and genuine well-wisher, you were brought into this world to accomplish a most impossible task. Somehow you were expected to transform our wretched selves—we who are most unqualified and who were once vigorously inimical to all of the royal principles of self-realization.

Dearest Srila Prabhupada, even today you remain a spiritual ambassador, fully commissioned by the Supreme Lord Himself to distribute so much love, mercy and compassion that you are empowered to save even such incorrigible and unsavable souls as myself.

Please do not give up on me, but continue to perform the miracle of making this insane soul sane. Please also keep reclaiming the other fallen, blinded and lost members of my family. Please forgive our dullness and our craziness. I am most unworthy. Still, I am sincerely begging that you continue to save me, even though I am an ungrateful receiver.

Chapter 6

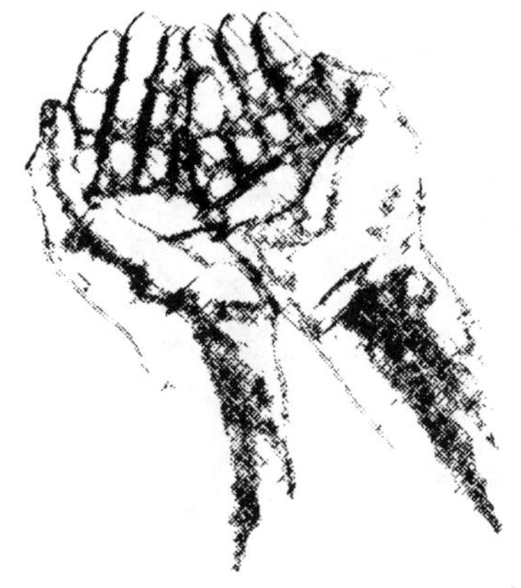

A Different Look At Eating, Sleeping, Mating And Defending

"I listened as this unusual civilization spoke a very peculiar language...To my amazement, all the conversations I overheard were about eating, sleeping, mating and defending."

A Different Look At Eating, Sleeping, Mating And Defending 47

Today my spiritual master had an extremely special lesson for me to learn. I had been feeling baffled as I tried to deepen my understanding of transcendental realities. Perhaps the intensity of my confusion is what caused him to give special attention to my concerns, for suddenly he appeared before me, all the way from another plane that is literally light years away.

"My dear son," he beckoned. "Please accompany me on a voyage. I know you have so much to say, but for now, just listen and observe." I stepped in place behind him and stood very still as we traveled to our first destination: the ocean. At first I was extremely frightened as he took me into the depths. But this fear was soon replaced with awe as I witnessed the unusual civilization that inhabited the ocean floor.

My spiritual master noticed my hesitant posture and began to calm me with his voice. "Fear not, my son," he said. "Simply listen and observe."

Taking his instruction, I listened. This unusual civilization spoke a very peculiar language, which, by my *guru's* mercy, I was able to understand. To my amazement, all the conversations I overheard were about eating, sleeping, mating and defending.

My *guru* then took me into the inner core of the earth. Again I was astonished to see another whole civilization—in fact, a totally different species—living so close to human civilization. Immediately I thought: How is it that these beings are so much a part of the earth's ecosystem and we know nothing of their existence? Hearing my thoughts, my spiritual master said: "There are actually many humans who know of these beings in detail. Just remember, right now your role is simply to listen and observe."

Again I noticed that all of these entities' speech and activities were centered around eating, sleeping, mating and defending. My *guru* said, "Study quickly, for we have thousands of environments to visit."

Next we went to several lower planets that were horrific and frightening. The bodily features of the beings were totally grotesque. I was afraid that if they saw us they would try to attack or harm us. But my *guru* proceeded fearlessly. "Simply listen and observe."

Within moments we were in the middle planetary system, and then later we traveled to the higher planets and even to other universes. I had never before seen so much opulence, heard so many languages or observed so many people engaged so intensely in varieties of eating, sleeping, mating and defending. The sights were astonishing. In the higher planets, each abode seemed more exciting than the last. Several times I wanted to ask my spiritual master if I could remain there, but before I could form the words he said, "Simply listen and observe."

Through mystic power, my spiritual master then allowed me to perceive all of these environments simultaneously. Seeing this was a total shock to my system. Still, by his grace, I noticed that every creature in all of these environments was intensely involved in making elaborate arrangements for eating, sleeping, mating and defending. By my *guru's* further grace, I soon realized how monotonous this program is. He also revealed to me how the end result of putting such great energy into these activities is merely death, old age, disease and disappointment; even the dumb animals are following the same routine.

I felt sorry for all of these entities—they were all so unaware of the futility of their efforts, and everything seemed so dry and meaningless. Then my spiritual master interrupted my train of thought.

"Now it is time for me to take you home to the spiritual world. But remember, you must promise to simply listen and observe."

When we arrived there, I was totally overwhelmed by spiritual sensations. Every molecule, every cell of the body I was inhabiting started screaming out in ecstasy. Suddenly, with no effort on my part, all of my senses became interchangeable and could perform the activities of any of the others. To my joyous disbelief, I could see with my ears and hear with my nose. I even tasted things with my eyes. The sensual stimulation I felt was a millionfold greater than that which I had experienced in other environments.

Now, more firmly than ever, my spiritual guide and master spoke gravely to me: "Even though it is very difficult, please just listen and observe."

This time I looked even more closely and, to my surprise, I saw the same exact pattern. Even here, all the residents were engaged in eating, sleeping, mating and defending. Only here there was no disease, old age or death, and everything in the environment was teeming with meaning.

Everything around me was alive, extremely vibrant, and eternally full of knowledge and bliss. The residents were eating, but simply for pleasure, not out of hunger. Moreover, as a service to the Divine Couple and each other, they all prepared colorful and magnificently fragrant foodstuffs.

The residents had no need for sleep, as they never tired or needed rejuvenation. Still, as another expression of their love, they would sleep in service to Lord Krishna just to dream and experience Him in another dimension.

Similarly, there was no need to mate to produce offspring, for conception would occur simply by their willing it. What's more, all of the sexual desires of these amazing entities could be satisfied by a single glance at the object of their senses. Still, these pure devotees would sometimes have union with one another, simply to enhance Krishna's pastimes and thus serve the Divine Couple in another expression.

The same was true of their defending. With no sense of proprietorship or insecurity, there was never any source of conflict. In fact, all of the residents knew unquestionably that everything belongs to the Divine Couple. Still, they would sometimes make a pretense of insecurity, anger or proprietorship, simply to intensify their adventures in service to the Divine Couple.

While I looked on at their ardent interactions, I heard my *guru* speak: "You are observing very nicely. It is not that in the absolute pure state there are no activities. Rather it is like the difference between a sane man and an insane man. Both of these persons are conscious and active, but the insane man's consciousness is unbalanced, unfocused and illusioned by temporary distortions. He therefore obscures the realities that surround him and does everything to avoid them.

"This is what you observed when you visited various material environments. In these places, the living entities are experiencing a form of insanity. Therefore, to the keen observer, their lifestyles are meaningless charades, full of limitations, impositions and sufferings. The saddest part is that they are thinking that they are enjoying, or will enjoy sometime soon, based on their future plans. But despite all of their efforts in these fields of limitation, the outcome is always the same. They are controlled by their senses and enslaved by eating, sleeping, mating and defending. Thus the ultimate consequence of all their actions is disease, old age and death."

I stood by him, at first saying nothing. "Do you fully understand everything that you have seen?" I nodded my head affirmatively.

"And what about your observations in the spiritual world? Were these also comprehensible to you?"

Now my face immediately registered my confusion, but before I could answer he said, "Of course, you cannot fully comprehend this, my child, but do not worry. One day, beloved, when you are able to return home for good, everything will become totally clear. For now, let us return to our own dwelling, for you have amassed sufficient information to infuse you with excitement about your divine future.

"One day soon, you will also be free to live in the realm of transcendence and blissfully serve our Divine Lords. Once you are completely free of the enslavement of your senses and totally unchained from the material environment, you will find yourself free from the demands of eating, sleeping, mating and defending. At that point, you will never again experience old age, disease or death.

"So keep listening and observing, my child. The next time I take you on a voyage, we will not be mere tourists. We will be returning home to our Divine worshipable Lordships to be in Their company forever. I am ready to take you back there now, but you are not yet ready to go. So improve on how you listen and observe. This is the key to breaking your bondage."

Chapter 7

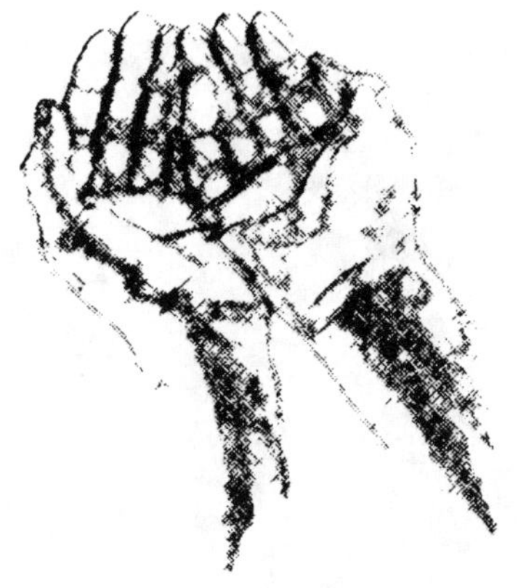

Advice To A Special Friend

"I feel the love of my spiritual mentors, and these personalities are the truest and greatest of lovers. Their love is so calming that it's as if I'm an infant being embraced to their bosom."

An associate of mine asked me yesterday why I was so happy and optimistic. He was extremely depressed and even exasperated by my jubilance. Eventually he even shouted at me: "How have you become so apathetic and insensitive? Or are you just naive? Don't you know that through biological and chemical manipulations, mankind is in a greater position to destroy human life than ever before in the history of this planet?"

My friend went on to explain that not only is there an abundance of nuclear weaponry, but now there are also massive levels of biological and chemical weapons in the hands of tyrants, so that even one mad terrorist could easily kill millions of people simply by releasing deadly chemicals into the atmosphere. "The aggressive and territorial attitudes of many so-called human beings have reduced three-quarters of the planet's people to the consciousness and behavior of animals," he screamed accusingly at me. "Don't you care about that?

"Just see!" he yelled. "Now women are having six or seven babies at a time, as if they were producing litters. That quantity of offspring is meant for insects and animals, not human beings. And all this is a result of biological manipulation."

I listened patiently to his tirade, not getting swept up in his passion. "How can you be so composed when millions of people this very moment are starving and homeless? While genocide is being committed in so many countries? When racism, homicide, suicide and incurable diseases are on the rise again at astronomical rates? Even people in extremely secure economic brackets are about to lose their jobs, their property and even their lives due to natural disasters.

"And what about the spiritualists?" I watched as he released his frustration. "What kind of solutions can they provide when everywhere you turn, they're having as much or more conflict and confusion in their own communities? Pretty soon there won't be any secure class of people except for the super-rich!"

"No. That's where you're wrong," I cut in. "The super-rich aren't secure; they only appear to be. But that's simply their own illusion. Actually, everything they do is ensuring that they will undergo severe chastisement for all their devious acts."

Finally I had his attention, and seeing that he was in profound need of hearing from me, I began to explain. "Yes, it's true that all that can go wrong is gradually going wrong, and, naturally, this is distressing to anyone who is closely studying these changes. But my special guides, my spiritual master and his agents, have given me ample notice and informed me about all these eventualities. They have told me exactly what to expect, and they have assured me that I can always reach out and connect with their soothing love, which is eternally available and encompasses not only me, but everyone.

"You see, these great masters have such large and active heart *chakras* that they are able to offer profound love and intervention to anyone who seizes the opportunity of their blessings."

Then I opened up to my special friend with an even deeper level of vulnerability. "Actually, my friend, on one level I am even more distressed and disappointed than you are about how the residents of this planet are suffering so intensely. But, on another level, I am extremely excited because I know that all of these sufferings are temporary, that they have karmic implications, and that they are ultimately part of the cleansing program.

"Often I am very lonely—so lonely I feel like I've been sentenced to live on an isolated island for eternity. But when I think of how my spiritual mentors watch over me at every moment and make themselves so easily available to me and to everyone, I become exhilarated to know that I am being divinely protected by such first-class associates.

"Often I feel so depressed and bound that nothing satisfies or entices me. I have no desire to go to bed, and once I fall asleep, I have no desire to wake up and face the emptiness of another day on this plane. But when I think about the exciting pastimes that eternally exist and await me and others in our original home in the spiritual world, my consciousness becomes surcharged and I feel absolute relief."

I looked deeply into my friend's eyes. "Often I become overwhelmingly angered at myself and others. I look for persons and situations to blame for all this chaos. But when I remember the words of my spiritual mentors about the importance of tolerance and compassion, those same events that engendered anger in me become catalysts for my personal development. In this way, I grow more expert in my ability to understand and appreciate myself and others, even in our imperfections.

"Often I study myself and others, and I am embarrassed by the degree of our selfishness. But when I think of all the sacrifices my spiritual master and the great *acharyas* made to release me from my prison, an overwhelming gratitude replaces all of my negative attitudes.

"I am one," I continued, "who is frightened by everyone and everything. Not only does the thought of war and calamities terrify me, but even a mosquito can disturb my equilibrium. But when I reflect on the numerous protectors I have who operate like divine angels, all of my fears gradually dissipate. And sometimes when I relax enough, I begin to realize just how hilarious my fearful state must be to these agents of the Lord, who see everything as Krishna's divine plan ultimately to help everyone.

"Sometimes I get totally disturbed by my finances. And this is occurring with more and more frequency. But when I realize how all wealth is controlled by God and His special agents, and how the real wealth of the devotee consists of his faith, austerity and spiritual resources, I become fully gladdened. I gratefully realize that I can increase these assets without limit, and use them whenever necessary without any depletion."

My friend listened attentively, almost dumbfounded by my candor.

"There are times when my health problems become so distracting that I feel incredibly useless, distressed and annoyed. But then I remember how many of the great spiritualists who preceded us and walked on this very planet had health problems of a proportion that totally dwarf my own. When I think this way, the small physical inconveniences I experience in my day-to-day struggles are no longer an obstacle to me, but instead become lively lessons and challenges for my growth.

"Of course, the realm of emotions is where I suffer most. I often feel extremely restless, like an energetic toddler who has been forced to sit in a corner and do nothing. The stillness feels agonizing. But when I begin to ponder the many activities that my spiritual mentors engage me in to help me and other souls advance toward them, I feel such thankfulness that I am compelled to find new ways to share with others all of the attention, love and knowledge they have given me.

"Sometimes I get so confused and bewildered when trying to deal with the myriad problems I face personally, socially, politically and economically, that I become almost catatonic. Sometimes I'm even momentarily rendered faithless because my problems are so bewildering. But at these extremely difficult times, I reconnect with my spiritual master and his agents, and their ever-available love and protection fully comfort and renew me.

"I know that you would also find joyous relief in my mentors' love, protection and guidance, because their presence eases all disturbances, and helps everyone in touch with them become fixed in equipoise. No matter what is going on in the material realm, my spiritual mentors invite everyone to take shelter of their calmness. And, like me, you can always be confident that they will be there for you without fail, especially when you need them most.

"My dear friend, these wonderful guides do not have biological families because their love and assistance are inclusive rather than exclusive. Their love is available to help everyone, but we must call out for their guidance. You see, they monitor everyone's desires, but it is only when our desires become singularly directed to them that we have the intensity to invoke their intervention.

"At that point—and at that point only—these masters will come running in response to your call. And this is why I am so enthusiastic. It is not that I am apathetic, insensitive or naive. I see, hear and feel all the same tragedies that are saddening you and keeping you off balance. It's just that I also feel the love of my spiritual mentors, and these personalities are the truest and greatest of lovers. Their love is so calming, it's as if I'm an infant being embraced to their bosom.

"My dear and special friend, this indescribably healing love is also available to you. So instead of continually analyzing and pondering the problems that are surrounding us, learn how to channel your energy into crying out for the masters' association. I assure you that when you do this with sincerity, you will become fully enlivened and refreshed—immune to and untouchable by any problem—and you will become extremely eager to receive more and more of such blessed fulfillment."

Chapter 8

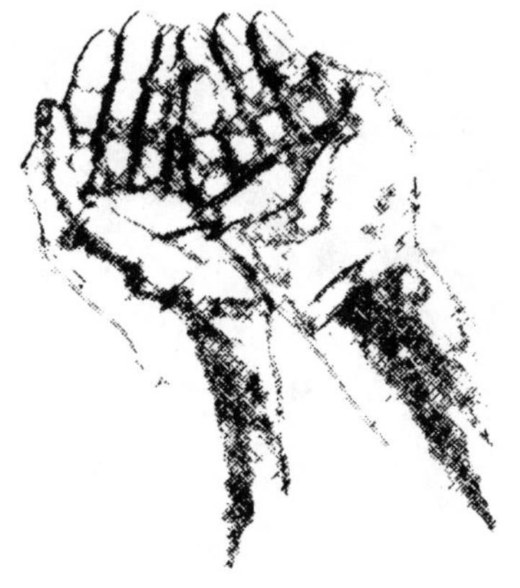

How Can A Strict Saint Be So Miserable?

"My spiritual master called for
me, but I could not come..."

Beloved Lord Damodara, I am a very spiritual person. I do not eat any flesh, take any form of intoxication, gamble or engage in illicit sex. Even though I am such a strict saint, my life remains unfulfilled. My spiritual master called for me, but I could not come—I was very busy reading his books. After all, I want to be the best philosopher, and unless I study his books most carefully, people will never recognize me as a scholar.

My dear Lord Damodara, I am a very spiritual person. I do not eat any flesh, take any form of intoxication, gamble or engage in illicit sex. Even though I am such a strict saint, my life is miserable. My spiritual master called for me, but I was not able to come—I was too busy singing his praises. Every day I sing songs of glorification to him. I think perhaps I should make a powerful record that thousands of people can hear, to help them understand what a great spiritual master my *guru* is.

My dear Lord Damodara, I am a very spiritual person. I do not eat any flesh, take any form of intoxication, gamble or engage in illicit sex. Even though I am such a strict saint, my life is full of setbacks. My spiritual master called for me, but I was not able to come, as I was too busy selling his books. My spiritual master has written volumes of books to help save the world. Many people know that I am an avid seller of his books, and so they are always approaching me to buy and distribute his different titles.

Dear Lord Damodara, I am a very spiritual person. I do not eat any flesh, take any form of intoxication, gamble or engage in illicit sex. Even though I am such a strict saint, my life is a shambles. My spiritual master called for me, but I could not come, for I was fully occupied in distributing spiritual food. There are many hungry people who wait in line to get a free meal. Some of them come daily, and most of them arrive hours before I come. When they see me pull up, many of them start cheering and applauding my valuable service.

Dear Lord Damodara, I am a very spiritual person. I do not eat any flesh, take any form of intoxication, gamble or engage in illicit sex. Even though I am such a strict saint, I am extremely unhappy. My spiritual master called for me, but I could not come because I was too busy attending various festivals. Every year there are so many relishable celebrations, so naturally I try to attend them all.

My dear Lord Damodara, I am a very spiritual person. I do not eat any flesh, take any intoxication, gamble or engage in illicit sex. Even though I am a strict saint, I am very morose. My spiritual master called for me, but I could not come because I was too busy chanting and dancing. When any congregational chanting starts, I am always there to lead. Often when others are leading, if people see me arrive, they invite me to take over. That is because my chanting and dancing inspire the entire temple room. When I am not there, things are rather dull.

My dear Lord Damodara, I am a very spiritual person. I do not eat any flesh, take any form of intoxication, gamble or engage in illicit sex. Even though I am such a strict saint, I am extremely dissatisfied in general. My spiritual master called for me, but I was not able to come because I was absorbed in preaching to the devotees. Preaching is the life and soul of a devotee. So every day I try to perfect my preaching. After years of doing this, I have become so expert that I can defeat any materialist. Sometimes just to entertain myself, I verbally chase away the impersonalists and frighten away mental speculators. The devotees often tell me how encouraged they are by my preaching, and this preaching keeps me fully engaged.

My dear Lord Damodara, I am a very spiritual person. I do not eat any flesh, take any form of intoxication, gamble or engage in illicit sex. Even though I am such a strict saint, I often feel like something is missing in my life. My spiritual master called for me, but I was not able to go because I was busy building temples for my *guru's* pleasure. Indeed, constructing gorgeous facilities that support my spiritual master's mission will make him very proud of me. Therefore, I am using the finest materials for this construction, and I will find the most expert and experienced architects. You see, I love my *guru* so completely that I will do everything in a very first-class manner just to be sure I thoroughly please him.

My dear Lord Damodara, I am a very spiritual person. I do not eat any flesh, take any form of intoxication, gamble or engage in illicit sex. Even though I am such a strict saint, I feel my life to be a failure. My spiritual master again called for me, but I could not go because I was so intensely engaged in establishing a self-sufficient community. The community that I envision will function like an embassy, for it will perfectly represent all of my spiritual master's noble ideas. The best way to truly glorify someone is to build a community based on the principles that person has taught. Since this is the highest glorification that can be given, everyone will see that I hardly have any time to do anything else, because I dedicate all my time to doing vital services for my *guru*. I am so busy, in fact, that I usually have to ask another godbrother or godsister to go and see just what my *guru* wants.

It's really incredible how such a small person as I can stay so busy in my spiritual master's service. The one thing I cannot quite grasp is how a saint as active and as strict as I am can possibly be so miserable. Perhaps you can help me understand this mystery—but not right now. You see, I have to get going. The new temple I'm building is about to have a ground-breaking ceremony and, as in so many of our major events, I am instrumental to the festivities.

Chapter 9

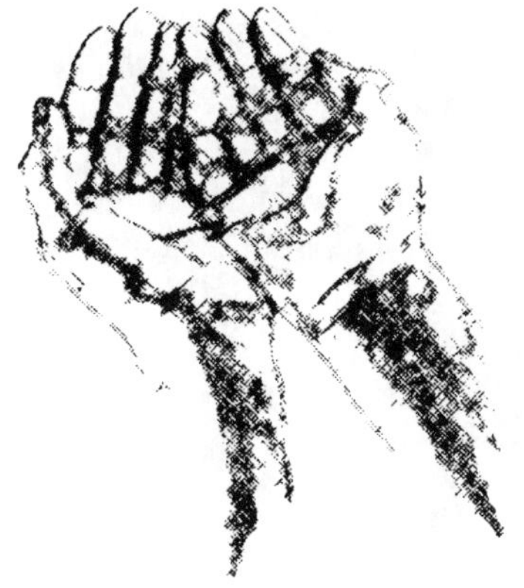

A Most Ungrateful Receiver

"You see, dearest Lord…I am always quick to look at what I think I need…but rarely at what You have already provided."

Dear Lord Shyama, simply by Your mercy, I am being offered one boon after another. I am embarrassed at how much You have given me, and how ungrateful I am.

I am traveling from village to village, city to city, and country to country, and miraculously, although I have no money, You are providing everything I need and an abundance of financial support.

Dear Lord Shyama, You have given me hundreds of disciples, and these disciples are as dear as my own children would be to me. This is quite amazing, given that renunciation in celibacy means having no offspring whatsoever, and no scope for procreating. How incredible it is that I had finally given up the idea of having a family, but then You gave me the grandest family of all.

My dear Lord Shyama, I do not drive automobiles, but You have given me many vehicles to take me to all kinds of preaching engagements. I have no car of my own, but by Your mercy, whenever there is need to travel, many vehicles are available for my use.

My dear Lord Shyama, I am without a permanent residence. But by Your blessing I have many homes. In all the countries I visit, there are wonderful temples I am able to stay in. As if that were not enough, I have many friends, disciples and well-wishers who compete in providing facilities to increase my comfort and resources.

My dearest Lord Shyama, I am the dullest of entities. I am slow and very inattentive. However, you keep surrounding me with wise people who supply me with causeless knowledge, even though I can hardly understand their complex concepts.

My beloved Lord Shyamasundara, it is in the department of social skills that I am most lacking. You see, I utterly lack charisma. I am such an introvert—noticeably devoid of vibrancy and creativity. But despite all of my deficiencies, You are making this poor fool popular. Such crowd appeal is dangerous for one such as me, whose ego is so easily inflated and who quickly thinks himself the proprietor. I therefore wonder how You can expect one like me, who receives so many boons for which I am not the least bit qualified, to remain grave and free of false identification.

When someone genuinely sacrifices to achieve a result, he feels a greater sense of appreciation, and is thus able to keep himself balanced and immune from false inflation. But surely it is impossible for a person so obviously unqualified to remain sober, secure and even-tempered when receiving reciprocation so far beyond my merit and ability.

Dearest Lord Shyama, each day You give me more and more, yet all the while I wonder how You can entrust me with increasing responsibility when I have already proven myself unworthy and immature. All of this baffles me because, as further proof of my insufficiency, I am constantly begging You for more blessings, although I can hardly cope with all that You have already given.

My dear Lord Shyama, You have given me a window to the spiritual world through which, by Your grace, I can gaze with little effort. Every day, You bestow the magnanimous opportunity for me to get glimpses of Your eternal abode. But rather than take advantage of Your munificent gift, I choose instead to focus my sight on the evidences of greed, lust and illusion that permeate the material world.

Most beloved Lord Shyamasundara, to assist me at every stage of life, You have continually sent precious living guides to mentor me, and many of these great souls have kept contact with me even after their passage. But instead of recognizing and accepting these mentors, I look for excuses to reject their expert, personal guidance. Therefore, despite the constant vigilance You have provided for me, I always wallow in my loneliness and complain of being neglected. My constant cries of loneliness are direct denials and rejections of Your love for me, yet you continue showering me with Your blessings.

My dear Lord Shyama, You have allowed me to walk through the door to freedom, even though I remain a self-made prisoner of my mind and senses. But now I have become confused and have entered a dangerous position. You see, fool that I am, I am apt to think that all the causeless blessings You have given me are actually my rightful claims. But in reality, it is obvious to everyone but me that these blessings are simply enticements You have given to induce this selfishly motivated businessman to become Your true devotee.

Lord Shyamasundara, please don't allow me to become proud of our connection, for if this were to occur, I would be doomed to eternal failure.

Dear Lord Shyama, I am the constant recipient of love flowing from You and the Divine Mother. Even my spiritual master, Your most noble, eternal servant, showers me with his attention. Still, I remain unappreciative of these gestures, and slow to reciprocate, but ever quick to offend.

My dear Lord Shyama, I can only beg that You will somehow or other continue to tolerate me just a while longer. You see, if You were to kick me away, I would have no other shelter or even justification for my existence. Even more frightening to me is the possibility that You might refrain from kicking me forward. You see, in this event there would be no real hope for my progress, for I am so intensely engrossed in false ego, sense gratification and self-centeredness that I would forever remain rooted in the land of vices.

Therefore, my dearest Lord Shyama, I beg You, although I am completely blind to it, please see the truth of my dependence on You. Despite all of my weaknesses, distractions and offenses, keep kicking me forward, and never kick me away from You, despite my fumbling attempts at service.

Indeed, I am a most ungrateful receiver, but You have spoiled me hopelessly, and now I am addicted to Your gifts. So please don't stop lavishing your attentions on me, and don't crush this illusion I maintain that I have actually won Your heart. You see, dearest Lord Shyamasundara, the truth is very plainly evident. I am always quick to look at what I think I need or don't have, but rarely do I look at what You have already provided. Therefore, once again, please forgive me for all of my improper behavior. It's just that I am ridiculously overtaken by this dull and ungrateful madness. Still, I beg You to overlook my many shortcomings, and never to hold me accountable for my ingratitude. Ingratitude is simply another symptom of my dementia, and without more of Your mercy, I have no hope for recovery.

Chapter 10

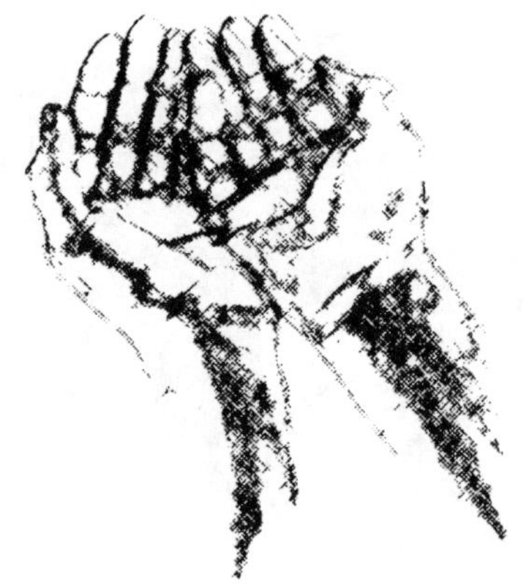

A Little Child Will Show You

"She turned
up to look at
me, and one
tear seemed to
freeze on her cheek as
she spoke…"

Today, as usual, I rushed to the temple room to make a few prayers before the Deities. I had been traveling for a few days, so I was most eager to see Lord Syamasundara. As I entered the temple room, I heard a sweet, melodious voice singing in the most lovely and penetrating way. It was the voice of a child, which gradually filled up every space in the temple, like the cool mist of frankincense swirling on the altar.

As the girl sang with powerful emotion, I wondered if I was intruding by entering this sacred space. She sang her prayerful song for Lord Syama as if offering her entire existence in that moment to the Deity. I stood in trance, intoxicated by the exchange between Lord Syama and this little girl.

I don't know how long I stood there, but when she turned around, I was shocked by her innocent beauty and her tear-filled lotus eyes. I asked her, "Little damsel, where have you come from? Who are the fortunate parents who have brought such an angel into this world?"

She stood silently, not answering, with a look that beckoned further inquiry, and so I continued: "Why are you crying, sweet damsel? Surely, you are far too young to know any kind of pain."

Again she said nothing, but instead turned away. My eyes followed her as she slipped through the door, back into the open space. Unable to forget the tears streaming down her face, I followed her to the temple stairs, where she was putting on her miniature moccasins.

"What's wrong, beloved? Please tell me; what has brought on these tears?"

This time she responded. "I am crying now because you rarely notice the tears in my eyes. The real question is 'Why are you adults so unconscious? Why do you leave me unprotected and give me so little while demanding so much?'

"You want me to be obedient, but how can I be obedient when all I see around me is mischief, anarchy and insubordination? You want me to be chaste, but most of the adults around me are constantly changing their mates and have had numerous wives or husbands. Some of them are openly promiscuous, although they wear the clothes of saintly persons.

"You say that I should give allegiance to an institution. But which institution should I be faithful to, and which branch of that institution? You adults have fragmented society so hopelessly that I am totally confused!"

I stood dumbfounded as she spoke. "You adults even go so far as to act as my fashion consultants and counselors. You tell me to dress less flamboyantly and be more grave in my attitude, but when I do adorn myself more modestly you totally overlook me! Why do you pretend to be concerned about my appearance when you don't really ever even see me?"

My heart burst as she continued. "When I cry to get your attention, you simply start chanting and praying louder, as if my concerns and my very existence are assaults on your peace of mind. You want me to dedicate myself to the mission, but where is the livelihood you are providing for me, and where is the example of steady commitment that can inspire me to take up this mission?

"You say you also want me to be a strong team player, and you view my efforts at individuality as mere ego. Why then don't you prove to me the benefit of teamwork through your own example?

"I hear you speak of unity, but I see from your own behavior that you only give this unity lip service, while in reality you pursue your own program."

Finally she turned up to look at me, and one tear seemed to freeze on her cheek as she spoke: "What I want to know, dear God-uncle, is this: Who are you kidding—me, Lord Krishna or yourself?"

Chapter 11

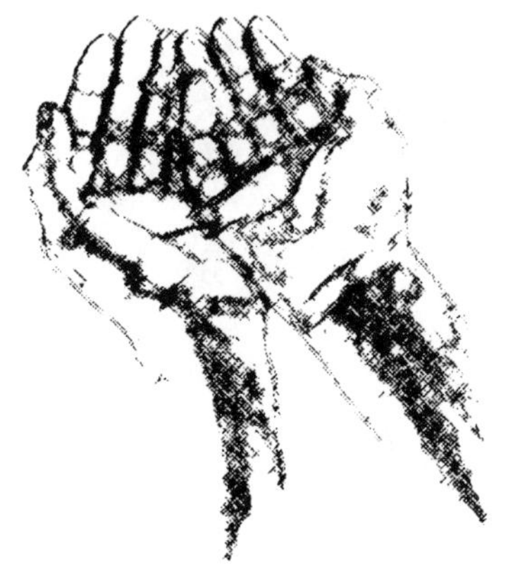

He Built A House The Whole World Can Live In

Dear Srila Prabhupada, please forgive my stubborn dullness, and please accept my most humble obeisances. All glories to your exquisite service.

Each year I become more and more amazed as I reflect on the wondrous qualities of the house you built for all humankind. Actually, your house provides shelter for every earthbound living entity, but you have kindly left the furnishing of this house up to us. I am nevertheless so dull that, although I live in so many of the magnificent structures you painstakingly labored to build, not only do I get distracted from my duty of furnishing them, but I often do things that are destructive to your gorgeous edifices.

For one thing, other devotees and I often forget to uphold the stipulations of our occupancy permit. Although we promised rigidly to follow the four regulative principles—the essential aspect of our tenancy agreement—many of us who dwell in your house have abandoned these liberating principles to again dabble in gambling, intoxication, illicit connections and the eating of meat, fish or eggs.

Pathetically enough, we also often try to take over each others' rooms, in an interplay of power politics. In acting out these impurities, we constantly find ways to exploit and manipulate each other in attempts to enlarge our own kingdoms. We even fight with each other about which floor we will live on, creating discord between the different *ashrams.* We create artificial gaps between the renunciates and the householders; between the women and the men; between the first-generation disciples and the second- and third-generation grand- and great-grand disciples. All of this is simply evidence of our immense immaturity.

Worst of all, we often leave small children in the house unprotected. That is to say, we put our children in *gurukula* school systems without arranging proper programs for them to have a strong, healthy and protected educational experience.

Of course, our tendency to waste your resources is also a conspicuous embarrassment. We unnecessarily leave the electricity and heat running all day long, and we waste so much money on lawsuits that should have been avoided. Because of this, you can rightfully call our whimsical spending habits concrete proof that we have made poor investments of your assets.

As if this were not enough, we also break the doors and windows of your house by not being sufficiently afraid of *maya. Maya* will attack the individual devotee as well as the community of devotees whenever and wherever there is an opening. When doors and windows are vandalized and destroyed, *maya* can very easily enter, and this is the condition in which we often leave your house.

Sometimes, we invite unhealthy guests into your house and then encounter serious trouble trying to boot them out. This occurs when devotees go outside of our devotional family and have unchaste association with other systems or with leaders of other systems. We should know better than this, and yet we often invite unworthy persons to come into your sacred residences and make themselves at home.

We also have another idiosyncrasy. Sometimes we only paint the outside of the house—as when we put great emphasis on public relations and on our external appearance, but do not properly care for individual devotees and the quality of their consciousness.

My dear Srila Prabhupada, the state of our front and back yards is also quite pathetic. We often let the grass grow wildly, engaging in hyperactive devotional service, but we refuse to remove the weeds. In this way, our devotional creepers get choked by the wild overgrowth of collective impurities.

As if this weren't bad enough, sometimes we even let parts of your house catch fire, destroying much of the wonderful mansion that you willed to us. This is of course the most dangerous of our offenses, because such fires seriously threaten the entire existence of your building and the total foundation that you have established. This occurs when we lose devotees en masse, and when we close down temples or preaching projects as a result of all the negativity we harbor.

Dear Srila Prabhupada, please forgive us for not properly maintaining what you have given us. Please empower us to move ahead and to complete the furnishing of the magnificent house that you have labored to build. The whole world is waiting to benefit from this creation. It is only due to our weaknesses that we have damaged and neglected this exquisite mansion in so many ways.

As seasoned heirs to your legacy who have made every error that can be made, we know that there is no better time than now for us to make the much-needed repairs to our inheritance. There is no better time than now to continue supplying the furnishings that will enhance the beauty of what you left behind in our care.

May all of us earnestly and vigorously do our parts, because it is certain that soon you will return to see the state of your house. Until then, I can only pray that we will quickly come up to speed so that when you return you will feel joyful pride in our contribution.

Chapter 12

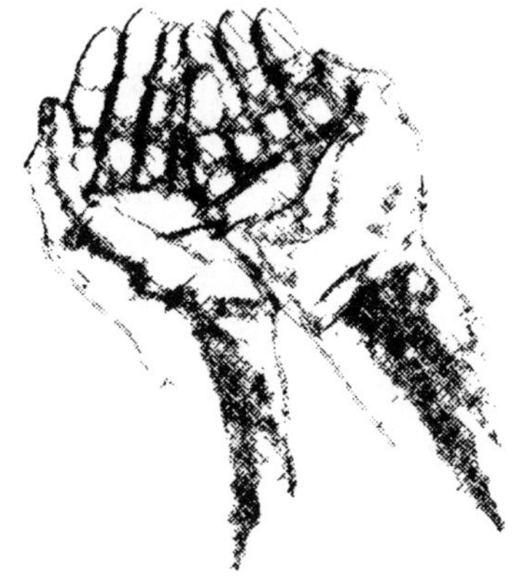

Standing At The Court Of Death

Death recently came and stole me away, like a thief snatching his prey in the dead of night. I found myself constantly thinking: "Why me? Why am I here of all places?" Days, months and years had gone by so quickly. I remembered being in primary school, high school, then college, and later traveling around the world. In my late forties, I had begun to feel some distinct changes in my body, but I had continued to live like I was immortal. I should have understood that those changes were signs of my machine wearing down.

Now, as I looked around, there was complete silence one moment, and then seconds later I heard loud screaming. A series of thoughts bombarded me. "Surely this noise will deafen me," I thought, "I've never felt so alone in my life." Then, moments later, I felt suffocatingly crowded in, as if I no longer had individuality.

At the height of my bewilderment, Lord Yamaraj, the fearsome Superintendent of Death, appeared, along with his court appointees. Instantly, I began shrieking at them: "This is a mistake. I am not supposed to be here!"

To my astonishment, all around me I could hear millions of other souls making similar, desperate pleas!

I tried to distinguish myself, to show that I was different, but each of the millions of souls around me had similar tactics. Although each of us was feeling that we did not belong in this courtroom, Lord Yamaraj somehow mysteriously addressed each person and explained to each of us why we had been brought before him.

Then Yamaraj looked directly at me and addressed me with stinging sarcasm. "You are

Bhakti-Tirtha Swami Krishnapada. Where is the *tirtha* of *bhakti*?" My mouth dropped open and I stood silently.

"Have you been able to get the souls under your care to take full shelter of you and give up their sinful habits? I think not!" He said. I could offer only a bashful shrug. "Didn't you know that if you could not and did not purify your dependents that you would be accountable for their sins? You have so many hundreds of sinners connected to you. Thus, you have huge quantities of debts to atone for. Even your own purity cannot save you now. What, then, do you propose?"

Again I said nothing. But then Yamaraj allowed me to study the scenes of my lifetime, and of many other lifetimes preceding it. I saw myself in and out of so many different bodies, like an actor in his dressing room trying on different costumes. In each body-costume, I would parade around for a few moments. But I noticed that in each body, no matter how different it was from the last, I felt completely at home and identified it as myself—often completely forgetting my mission.

Even during times when I had some clear power of recollection, the surrounding environment would have such an impact on me that I would frequently become acculturated. As I studied these previous lives of mine, it seemed foolish that I had become so absorbed in my distractions and superficialities. It was even more ridiculous how I tolerated so much nonsense from those under my care, as if negative situations would just blow away. In every life there was much assistance available to help me tune into the spiritual world, but I was so carried away with each costume and backdrop that I kept neglecting the obvious.

Then suddenly I sped up to this lifetime, to examine it more carefully. This time, I had even more divine help than in my previous lives, but still the distractions were many. I looked again at Yamaraj and tried to formulate a defense. In a cracking voice, I said: "I chanted my sixteen rounds every single day and never broke any of the four regulative principles."

King Yamaraj turned to his assistant. "Explain things to this pretender."

The assistant turned in my direction. "It's true, you chanted daily, but your chanting was more for liberation than for unmotivated, selfless service." The knot in my throat rippled. "You also followed the four regulative principles: ate no flesh, took no intoxicants, and didn't gamble or engage in illicit sex life. But in your mind you constantly broke the principles." He paused. "It's time you understood how the law works; so pay attention! Your physical body changes every lifetime, but your mind carries your actual self to its next existence; thus you are accountable for all these mental deviations."

"But what about all the service I did?" I exclaimed with smug certainty.

"Do you think that the service of your ego constitutes devotional service? Throughout all your grand service, your greatest interest was your own fame. And now, you have achieved that success you were chasing, for you are very famous here amongst the infamous."

"But I have a powerful spiritual master," I

challenged. "Surely you're aware of Srila Prabhupada!"

"You're right. And this is another reason you have been sent here. You see, to assist you and others, Lord Sri Krishna personally sent you one of His topmost special agents. Srila Prabhupada was Krishna's specially empowered representative, directly connected with Lord Chaitanya Mahaprabhu and Lord Nityananda Prabhu. Just to help the likes of you, Lord Krishna sent His Divine Grace Srila Prabhupada to that wretched environment you dwelled in. Srila Prabhupada was the *senapati bhakta*—a great field commander who would go to every corner of the world to reclaim souls. But even though Krishna sent such a great soul to assist all of you, neither you nor the others properly honored him or fully submitted to his desires. Eventually, Lord Krishna felt that Prabhupada was overstaying, and therefore He called him back, although he was willing to continue helping you ungrateful souls."

Yamaraj's assistant continued. "Actually, in the end it was the sins of his unqualified disciples that brought Srila Prabhupada's body down so fast. You disciples must take responsibility for his early departure. In fact, persons like you must be dealt with on two levels. You will have to bear the burden you caused your spiritual master with your own weaknesses, and you will also have to carry the weight of your disciples' sins."

My heart sank to my toes as he asked: "Which of these areas do you want to suffer for first?"

At first I was speechless, but finally I managed to speak. "Please punish me first for those burdens I caused my *guru*."

As soon as I said this, Lord Yamaraj Himself reappeared, but this time He was weaponless. "You, my dear, are most fortunate," Yamaraj said. "Having pity on you, your spiritual master has intervened and summoned me to give you release." Before I could reply, he continued. "Even we are amazed at how your *guru* is willing to absorb more of your karmic reactions. This kind of compassion is something we rarely, if ever, see."

Then I heard my spiritual master's voice. "You do not belong there. Come with me, my beloved child, so that we can be together again."

"But Srila Prabhupada, I am not worthy of you."

"It doesn't matter," he answered.

"But—" I resisted.

"Don't you know that at the ceremony in which you took second birth, I agreed to become your father?"

Although I wanted to, I could not speak. "My son, there is no abandonment in the spiritual world, nor are there any neglected children. Liberated spiritualists have no such dysfunction," Prabhupada said to me. "Besides, my son, our connection is eternal."

With these words, I bowed at Srila Prabhupada's feet. And when he leaned over and touched my head, contact with his fingertips caused me to spiral in unparalleled ecstasy. Suddenly, I thought of just how unworthy I was of my *guru's* unending compassion; then I lost consciousness.

Chapter 13

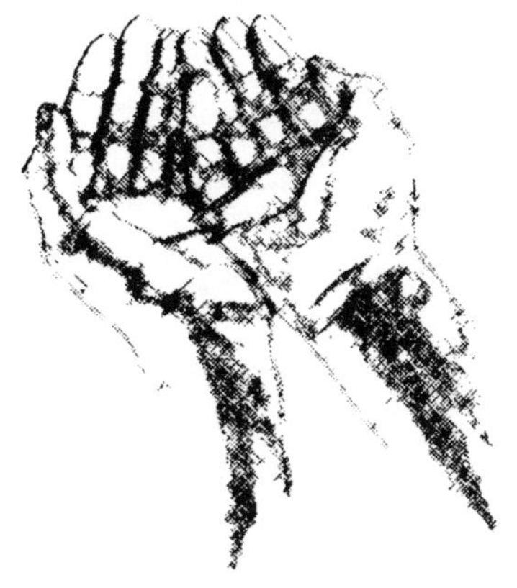

Earth Changes Give New Meaning To Life

Earth Changes Give New Meaning To Life

Only a few years back, so many of my ideas and plans seemed to be so important and so easily attainable. If only I had truly accepted what was most obvious, I could have lived a much more meaningful life. Perhaps I could have even glimpsed eternity.

I had plans for becoming a great scholar, writing many books and giving riveting lectures to large audiences at universities. But now that the earth has shifted on its axis, most academic institutes are merely piles of rubble. Even worse, I now realize how much of what we were studying and teaching was simply information processing and data collection—not the sharing of truth and wisdom.

Among my colleagues, I was considered politically astute, and was totally at home with current affairs. On any issue, I could organize and lead campaigns or act as an advisor. But now that the earth has shifted on its axis, none of these secular strategies offers any benefit.

Of course, I have always considered myself to be a renaissance man. Thus, in preparation for my material ascent, I would spend many hours a day practicing my music. People loved to hear me perform, for I was one of the world's greatest musicians. In fact, I would often merge with my instrument and play it as if we were one. Naturally, with all of this talent, I would practice every chance I got. But after the earth shifted on its axis, many musicians like myself became aware of how we had helped degrade the previous civilization by projecting lower sound vibrations onto the planet and increasing everyone's tendency toward passion.

Because I also worked hard to maintain my appearance, almost everyone envied my wonderful physique. After all, I was a well-rounded athlete with outstanding health. Being naturally competitive, I had the perfect mindset for winning. Needless to say, I practiced hard to be the best athletic performer in all sporting events, and I often succeeded. But when the earth shifted on its axis, I personally saw hundreds of thousands of people leave their bodies in hardly more than an eyeblink. Thousands were claimed by earthquakes, floods, famines and diseases, while many others fell prey to the rash of sudden, sporadic wars. Finally it became clear to me how temporary the material body is, that everyone will have to give it up sooner or later, and that the transition is often not an easy one.

My wife and children were so dear to me that gradually I began to dedicate every moment of my life to their happiness and security. I became so attached to them, in fact, that I actually convinced myself I was their invincible protector. But when the earth shifted on its axis, I had to watch each member of my family succumb to terrifyingly horrible suffering as they were victimized by the plague.

Of course, my greatest diversion was the lifelong effort I put into building my very own dream house. I envisioned this as a fantastic palace near the ocean. I first found some perfect beachfront acreage and then I enlisted the finest architects to draw up plans. Everything went wonderfully, and I was ready to move into my earthly paradise after just one or two more features were added. But when the earth shifted on its axis, in minutes my dream house and many others crumbled into sawdust. Swept up by a swift current, my beautiful palace just floated away from me like a light piece of timber, and I was totally devastated.

All this seemed like a frightening nightmare to me. I remember meeting with some of the world's top investors. These global economists steered me to the most guaranteed investments—ones they assured me were practically risk-free. On their account, I believed that if my other plans fell through, I would always have my mutual funds to fall back on. I never imagined that our civilization would be so devastated that even bank accounts, CDs and stocks would no longer be of value.

Still, there was no dearth of fantasy in my life. One of my favorite fantasies was my dream of retiring early. My fail-proof plan was that I would use my pension and social security payments to support me while I traveled, carefree, around the world. I pictured myself always eating in the best restaurants and visiting many famous sites. But ever since the earth shifted on its axis, food itself has become so scarce that, except for those who are growing their own food, most people are starving. As for visiting historical sites, none of this matters any more. Now that the entire planet has been restructured, whole land masses have sunk into the ocean while others have risen out of the sea as unrecognized protrusions.

Before the cataclysms, there were many emphatic warnings from scientists, mystics and psychics. There were even mass dreams from all bona fide religious traditions and from native people of many ancient cultures. Most important was the warning from my own spiritual master, who often spoke of impending danger and the fall of modern civilization.

I do not know how I was so foolish as to go on every day, not preparing economically, sociologically, psychologically or even spiritually for what everyone said was inevitable. What baffles me most is this: out of so many millions of people who also didn't take the warnings seriously, why was I blessed to be one of the survivors?

Then out of nowhere my spiritual master appeared and started to speak. "Yes, beloved. It is good that you are reflecting on how you were so absorbed and attached to the temporary material world. In this way, you can seriously grow from the mistakes you made in your former life, just before the cataclysms. You see, beloved, you actually did not survive the disaster. You were so very materially attached and intoxicated that, until the very end of existence, you stayed right in the eye of the storm, certain that your fallible soldiers would protect you. You were taken so quickly it was almost painless. Still, because you have performed a significant degree of devotional service in this lifetime, I was obliged to arrange some protection for you in proportion to the genuineness of your love and surrender. I therefore placed you in this environment, so you would have facility to continue in your struggle for liberation.

"I will no longer be able to be with you physically, as I was before the devastation, but know that I will always send help for you when you are truly ready for it. Everything that has happened to the people on this planet is due to consciousness. As you and those around you change your consciousness, help will be sent accordingly.

"It would have been easier for you to obtain liberation while I was physically present with you," he continued, "and far easier to return home back to Godhead. However, the suffering you witnessed and are experiencing now will give you great strength and determination. Now I must go," he said, "I have many other obligations to meet."

I cried out and begged: "Please don't leave me behind!" But he had already disappeared.

Chapter 14

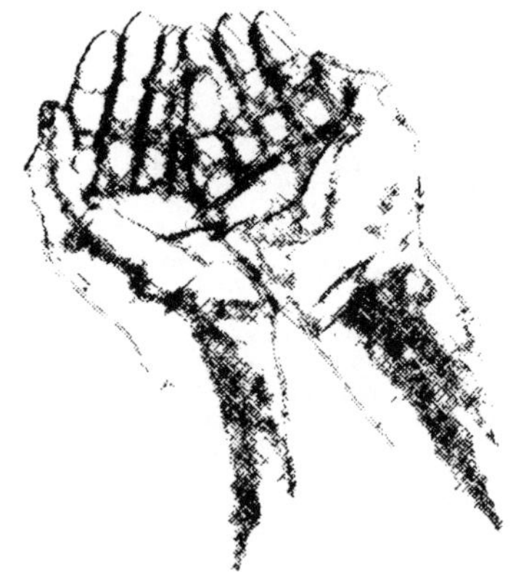

One Day At A Time

"My dear Lord, I therefore beg You please to tell me: Is there really any difference between the recovering alcoholic and me?"

Dear Lord, is there really any difference between me and the recovering alcoholic? In the beginning, the alcoholic spends years in denial of his addiction, feeling that he is in control and can check his drinking any time he desires. But how do I really differ? You see, I am the one who has been in denial—not for years—but for hundreds of lifetimes. I have continually taken shelter of my weak constitution, thinking myself to be in utter control. But when it comes to cleansing the garbage that resides in my mind, I remain at a total loss.

My dear Lord, I therefore ask You, is there really any difference between me and the recovering alcoholic? The alcoholic is always thinking about his past adventures with intoxication. He often longs to experience that taste again, but is totally frightened of the consequences. If he avoids alcoholic beverages, it is not out of any self-mastery or discipline, but only out of cowardice. It is simply because he is too afraid of the consequences associated with alcohol.

Then there is me, the so-called devotee. The seeds of sinfulness are deeply embedded in my consciousness and, even though I don't externally engage in such behaviors, past desires are always there to haunt me. Every day, I strain to ignore them, but the ghosts of these desires linger lazily in my heart, and never fully go away.

My dear Lord, I therefore beg You please to tell me—is there really any difference between me and the recovering alcoholic? When former alcohol abusers associate too intimately with one another, they sometimes resume their enslavement to the substance. Collectively and individually, they begin to worship it, meditate on it and think incessantly about various intoxicants. When separated from the bottle even for a moment, they begin to feel as if that separation were lasting for more than a decade.

My addiction was to the cinema. I remember how, not very long ago, I would go to a video store and come home with hours' worth of movies. Just one night without a video would feel to me like an extended jail term. Therefore, I ask you, dear Lord, is there really any difference between me and the recovering alcoholic?

The former drinker tries to reject everything unfavorable to his sobriety, and he eagerly embraces everything that supports it. But all the while he forgets that the great majority of his existence is unfavorable, because a life of continuous fear and struggle to avoid old patterns and old associates is in itself a hellish challenge. I, too, am in this predicament because I must avoid so much of what used to bring me pleasure, now that I realize how incarcerating these activities are.

What then, O Lord, is the difference between me and the recovering alcoholic, who goes through his day upholding a pretense of normal behavior? Although on the outside he appears to be coping, in that part of him that no one sees, he is internally crying out and struggling because his addiction has suppressed all other desires. Even when he appears to have a happy expression, inside he is terrified of the mood shifts he knows might overcome him if some activity plugs him back into his old patterns.

Dearest Lord, I thus honestly beg You please to tell me—is there really any difference between me and the recovering alcoholic? For former drinkers, some days seem to go on endlessly, and just waking up the next morning is almost impossible. Throughout the day, these ex-addicts face struggles and challenges at every step, only to meet similar challenges the very next day and the next.

As former drinkers look to the future, sometimes all they have to look forward to are the adversities of more and more tests. These recovering alcoholics travel around and explain to current addicts how their Higher Power has allowed them to give up alcohol, and how others can accomplish this arduous task. Recovering alcoholics even boast of being sober for five, ten, twenty, or even twenty-five years. Still, no one knows more than they do that these decades seem like only yesterday, and that just one sip from a shot glass can unravel all of their progress. One sip can make them once again install a wine or whiskey bottle on the altar of their consciousness and make this bottle their worshipable deity.

Dear Lord, it was Your great message carried by Your dedicated messengers that ultimately cleansed my heart and pulled me out of the gutter. But how will I be able to avoid going back into a gutter mentality that could eventually degrade me into a gutter existence once again?

It was then that I heard the voice of my sweet Lord's servant chuckle tenderly and non-judgmentally at my awkward predicament. The voice was female and full of loving emotion.

"My cherished beloved," she said. "Just like your friend, the recovering alcoholic, you must learn to take things one day at a time. Temptations are there, but just as you have overcome them so many times in the past to get this far, you must continue warding off these demonic desires to achieve complete mastery of your spiritual technology.

"Now, my child," the melodious voice continued, "maintain and persevere. In fact, enjoy your success rather than lamenting your challenges. You have applied for an advanced degree—of course there will be demanding tests that you will have to pass. However, my precious one, you can rest assured that if you keep sincerely endeavoring to maintain your material sobriety, you will very soon be invited by our Divine Master to thoroughly enjoy spiritual intoxication!

"Unfortunately for you, you are not yet thirsty enough for this position, and so there have been delays in your ascension. But I have confidence that soon you will be very thirsty and eager for this attainment.

"Until that time, just remain firm and fixed in your new lifestyle and go more deeply into your realizations. Do not waste even a moment on extraneous activities. Be very attentive, and avoid all associations that in any way weaken your resolve. And know for sure that we are guiding you. We are all indescribably intoxicated on love of God! But we will be even more blissful when you come and join the eternal party with us and all of your liberated loved ones.

"Always remember that we love you dearly, and that there is no shame in wanting intoxication. Just never settle for the imitation intoxication of the material dimension. Instead, always hanker to partake of the real sweetness of spiritual inebriation by embracing the actual altered state that exists in pure love of God. This can and will come effortlessly, but only when you unhesitatingly love and serve our Supreme Master and dance wildly for His pleasure.”

Chapter 15

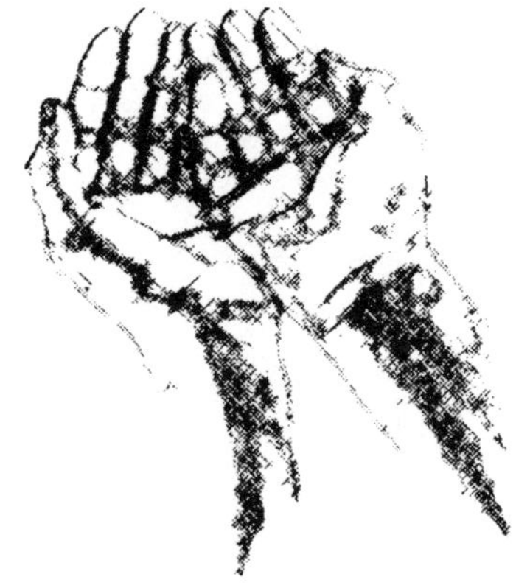

A Transcendental Playground

"My dear Lord Damodara, why are You running away from me? I have tried so hard to catch You and worked so hard to earn Your association. You promised me that if I pleased You, You would be all mine and I would be all Yours. I gave You the best years of my life—almost my entire young adult life. Now I'm getting older, and in this lifetime I will never again experience the vitality of youth."

Lord Damodara mischievously taunted me as He ran further and further away. "Do you think I can be tricked by years of poor-quality service? Or by service that is begrudging? It is not quantity that pleases Me, or even quality, but the attitude of the server," He teased cunningly.

"But, my dear Lord Damodara, don't run from me. Don't you realize I gave up my entire pursuit of mundane education, and I abandoned my career, just to devote full attention to the study of Your pastimes? If anyone did, I gave rapt aural reception to the hearing of these pastimes among Your devotees. After all, You have said that one who knows the transcendental nature of Your appearance and disappearance in the material world does not return to this dimension."

Again, the Lord corrected me, this time picking up speed. "Knowing Me is not an intellectual endeavor. Real knowledge is appreciating the necessity of full surrender and acting on this knowledge accordingly."

"My dear Lord Damodara," my voice followed him. "Please slow down; do not run away from me so vigorously. Don't you know that I gave up all my affiliations with churches, mosques and mystery schools to become a full-time student of *bhakti yoga*? The choirs in many of those churches made my heart swoon. I loved the simplicity of the mosque and was fascinated by metaphysics."

Lord Damodara laughed. "You think I don't know that Your greatest devotion is to your own prestige and glory? You were ready to do anything to receive glorification, even worship Me. But just tell me, which of the many austerities you performed was not actually done for fame? Actually, you became a first-class devotee of self-adoration. Now, do you really think that someone so distracted by all this distinction can ever capture Me?"

"My dear Lord Damodara, how can You watch me suffer in this way? Every time I'm about to catch You, again You dart away. Don't You know that I have deliberately ignored and disappointed all of my relatives in favor of serving You? Where is Your reciprocation? You're simply ignoring me."

At these words, the Lord's voice strengthened. "Better than avoiding and ignoring suffering souls is being potent enough to engage them in My service. But until you engage yourself with genuineness and generosity, no one will be inspired to appreciate your dedication."

"But, my dear Lord Damodara, I gave up my fiancée and took a lifelong vow that I would always live alone, without a partner. I even took a lifetime vow of celibacy, agreeing to avoid even sex life designed for procreation."

This line seemed to amuse Lord Damodara the most. "So you have given up one fiancée and stopped mating. But how many fiancées have you considered in your fallen mind? And how frequently did you imagine yourself mating? Besides, you of all persons should know that I Myself am sex life performed according to religious principles. Mating, therefore, is a most wonderful service for those who can produce devotees."

A feeling of total dejection entered my heart. "My dear Lord Damodara, You have exposed my true self to me, and convinced me that I have simply served on an external level, with very little substance. I even understand now that it is Your grace alone that has enabled me to meet the many demands of my rigid renunciation—an austerity that You so kindly give me credit for. What baffles me is why so many of my spiritual children are also suffering. Is it because of my weakness that you are also running away from them? These dear children seemed to me to be the special helpers that my godbrothers and I prayed for. You sent them to us, but now You have taken many of them back, and this is extremely painful to all of us. Please, Lord Damodara, tell me why this has happened!"

Lord Damodara came to a sudden halt. "My dear child, at your present speed, you will never catch up to Me. And so I keep trying to send you help, but you are so dull and impotent that you are even too slow to connect with this help. This leaves Me only one alternative. I have been forced by My love for you to send a few advanced runners to help you and your colleagues create a compassionate and selfless loving environment that will prepare all members sufficiently to receive the help of My great emissary-generals.

"Beloved, you want to catch Me, bind Me and make Me all yours. But I am more eager and determined to make you Mine than you can imagine. Therefore, honor these youthful souls that I have temporarily removed from your presence. They are under My care and many of them will soon return to you in new forms.

"I and these souls have exchanged incredible instances of intense love," little Lord Damodara continued. "With the love they have given Me and the love I have returned to them, we will soon all capture one another."

The Lord then stooped down like a child racer about to sprint away. "Now I must run on. But tell the elder leaders and other members of the community that they must treat all children as if they had sprung from their very own loins. You see, this is more true than they can ever hope to know. These children, after all, are My eternal playmates. It is I Who have sent them to you, and it is I Who will determine when either you or they will leave the earth plane and return to My transcendental playground.

"Beloved, please hasten to rejoin Me. There is so much fun, adventure and love waiting here for you. There are so many friends you can laugh and play with eternally. So speed up, and stop settling for temporary distractions. Beloved, nothing will ever satisfy you except for reuniting in play with Me."

Chapter 16

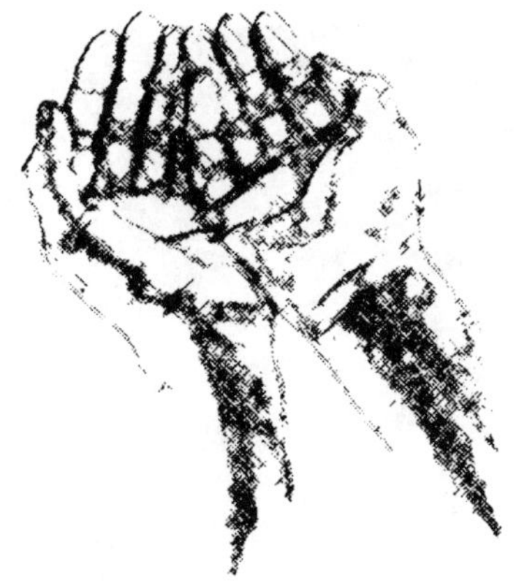

Well Done, My Darling, Well Done

"With each person
I encountered,
I only discussed
devotional topics
and personalities.
Therefore, I was
feeling constantly
enlivened as I
reflected on all of
the glorious beings
in my life."

Today I practiced mindful breathing. As I inhaled, I imagined drawing in love, serenity, knowledge and bliss. As I exhaled, I imagined releasing lust, anger, fear and sadness. When I entered the temple and I looked at your picture, I saw you smile at me and say, "Well done, my darling, well done."

Today when I went out, I practiced mindful walking. I walked for hours—I passed many people and saw many things. I sometimes had to avoid the danger of cars, dogs and obstacles on the road. Nevertheless, I felt that the sun was shining to infuse my body with dynamic energy, and that the birds were chirping just to cheer me on and encourage me toward my destination. Later on, when I returned to the temple, I looked at your picture and saw you smile at me and say: "Well done, my darling, well done!"

Today I practiced mindful talking. I was extremely careful not to say anything to offend anyone. I imagined that each word was showering another soul either with flower petals or with bricks. Devotional words are like flowers that will enhance another's well-being and celebrate that person's existence. Harsh or whimsical words are like assaults on others, as if stoning them with bricks.

With each person I encountered, I only discussed devotional topics. Therefore, I was feeling constantly enlivened as I reflected on all of the glorious beings in my life. Later, when I returned to the temple, you smiled and again repeated: "Well done, my darling, well done."

Today I practiced mindful hearing. I reflected on how all conversation is a call to participate in certain activities or to accept certain mindsets. I chose to participate exclusively in devotional activities, and I only wanted to reflect on devotional topics. Thus, whenever there were discussions that did not invite me to participate in devotional activity or reflection, I would simply excuse myself from the environment.

I even went out of my way to seek the association of those who invited me to glorify the *gurus*, *sadhus* and the Divine Couple, and I consciously avoided the association of those who tried to entice me away from Their love and shelter. When I returned to the temple, I noticed your picture smiling as you said, "Well done, my darling, well done."

Today at the breakfast table, I practiced mindful eating. First, I thought of all my wonderful disciples who so conscientiously prepare foodstuffs for the pleasure of the Lord and myself. They always punctually prepare these meals in a clean, devotional mood and atmosphere. After carefully considering their service, I reflected on how the meal had been lovingly offered in prayer to the Supreme Lord, and how, later on, the Lord's remnants were made available for others.

As I chewed each morsel, I thought of how each preparation was now spiritually surcharged, and that by taking such foodstuff, my body was being fueled with spiritual nourishment. Then I thought of how each grain, each mouthful, was giving me the power to improve the quality and quantity of my meditation and service. After honoring this spiritual feast, I went into the temple, and there you were. Once again, your lips were curled in a smile, and you said to me "Well done, my darling, well done."

Today I practiced mindful seeing. I reflected on how all things are composed of different energies of the Supreme Lord—that is, either His superior, marginal or separated energies. This allowed me to feel Lord Sri Krishna's presence constantly. Then I made a point of reflecting on the fact that everything I observed was coming from Krishna, and should be offered back to Him.

Gradually, I recognized everything in creation as being a part of the Lord's universal form. Thus, things I would normally see as uninteresting, grotesque or frightening began to take on a far more meaningful appearance. Sights that ordinarily engendered lust or fear in me no longer bothered me. Instead of seeing them as objects for my enjoyment, I saw them all as aspects of the Divinity.

With this new vision, I understood all captivating members of the opposite sex to be transformations of Krishna's beauty, and I no longer felt resentful of their radiance or inappropriately attracted to them. Soon, I adopted this attitude toward everything that spoke to my senses. Instead of getting agitated by trying to enjoy an experience, I saw each subject or environment that allured me as a display of Krishna's splendor. Later, when I returned to the temple and looked at your picture mindfully, I saw you beam an effulgent smile and nod, "Well done, my darling, well done."

Today I practiced mindful reading. As I perused different scriptures, I no longer read as if scanning a novel or ancient history, nor did I read as if studying mere philosophy or theology. As I read each chapter, I saw every section as a peephole into the spiritual realm. Then I would study the subject more closely and reflect on all the phenomenal activities taking place in the spiritual kingdom.

All of a sudden, before I could stop myself, I began to weep incessantly, because I understood that no matter how much I pondered these writings, I was not yet qualified to interact with these great entities. Nor could I fully comprehend them, communicate with them or participate in their pastimes of adding to the Supreme Lord's pleasure.

All this made me feel incredibly unfortunate as I pondered the irony of coming so close to the spiritual world, yet still remaining so far from its residents. I wept in agony, thinking: "Why have I been brought to the dinner table, but then not been allowed to eat? How could I be brought to the very tip of the window, but then only allowed to window shop? What is the value of all these mindful practices," I cried, "if I must continue my existence in this gross, material body?"

I went to the temple and again looked at your picture. This time you were not smiling, but you were also crying, and this made me cry even more. Only now, to my incredible delight, you stepped right out of your picture and came up and gently embraced me. Then you looked compassionately into my eyes and spoke:

"In your mindful breathing, walking, talking, hearing, eating and seeing, I was always with you.

When we returned to the temple I smiled each time, knowing that you were shedding all the obstructions that have bound you to the material plane. I was smiling also because I so greatly enjoy your association during these mindful meditations. You see, at these times we connect on a far deeper and more wonderful level. So, my darling, there is no reason for your sadness. Don't become so easily discouraged. As long as you maintain your mindful platform, I am mindful of you! More importantly, when you learn to practice mindful sleeping, you will be able to fully connect with me, because then you will be able to understand one of the most sublime cosmic secrets: Throughout the day, while your body is active, you are actually in a deep slumber. It is while your body is at rest during the night that you are actually more awake.

"At present, in your day-to-day affairs, you are almost fully asleep, but you are gradually waking up. So, my darling, please go into a very deep and mindful sleep—for in this state, we will be able to meet and communicate like never before.

"I have so much to tell you, so much to show you, and even more to share with you. So wipe away your tears of sadness. In the near future, there will be time and reason for shedding an ocean of tears. But these will not be tears of pain. They will be tears of pure, ecstatic joy."

With these words, you jumped back into your picture, only this time your smile was bigger than ever. When you spoke, you said "Don't ever forget mindful sleeping, for it is through this mindful state that you will be awakened from your stupor of illusion and confusion. For now, just carry on with your mindfulness, and know that I am eagerly awaiting you, for yours has been a job well done, my darling, well done!"

I stared for several moments at your picture. Later that night, I heard your voice faintly repeating, "In all your activities, always aim for mindfulness. And especially aim for mindful sleep."

Chapter 17

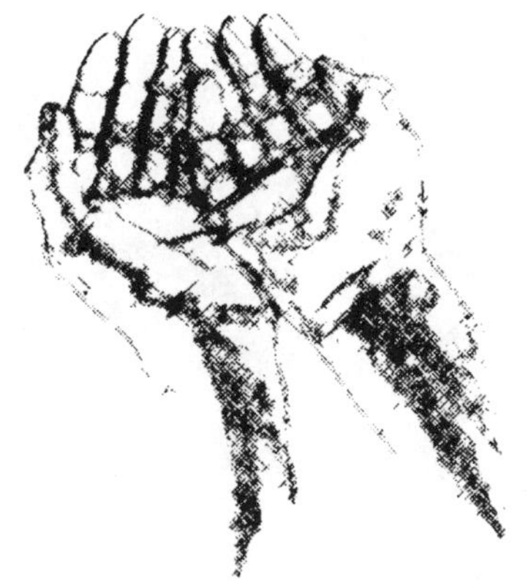

Please Teach Me The Language Of The Heart

"To reach You,
I mustn't
communicate
through my
hands, mouth,
ears or eyes, but
I must speak to
You through my
heart."

Please Teach Me The Language Of The Heart 125

My dear Lord Paramatma, I have made a great effort to visit many holy places of pilgrimage. I have traversed long distances to walk on sacred ground, take holy water and garner spiritual souvenirs. At these holy places, I always imagine how Your pastimes are performed, and I try to envision the activities of Your associates in relation to these pastimes. But, although trying to understand clearly what has happened in these sacred areas in order to see and love You more fully, I felt myself a failure.

My dear Lord Paramatma, I have often gone to mystics and psychics to discover secret formulas to control my senses, develop extraordinary powers and defeat all of my enemies. But in doing this, I found that these formulas did not allow me to see You and love You more fully, and so I felt myself a failure.

My dear Lord Paramatma, I have very diligently practiced chanting mantras, taking them from many traditions. I have used Christian, Islamic, Buddhist, Zen, Tantric and Vedic mantras. Some of these mantras were extremely difficult for me to pronounce, and many were only to be chanted under very special conditions. Some were even forbidden to be revealed to anyone, although some instructors would secretly impart them to earnest students. These mantras had numerous purposes, such as invoking peace and obtaining protection. But after chanting them, and finding You still absent, I felt myself a failure.

My dear Lord Paramatma, I even took special linguistic courses in order to read the scriptures in their original languages. Since English is such a materialistic language, I thought that if I could only read ancient texts in the spirit of their original tongue, all their mysteries would be revealed to me. But after my long and arduous linguistic study—finding that I was still not fully seeing or loving You—I felt myself a failure.

My dear Lord Paramatma, I have performed so many austerities—depriving myself of food, sleep and even liquids. Sometimes I would go whole days on just two or three hours of sleep. Many days I totally fasted or ate only fruit. Very often my head would grow light and I would have great difficulty with my body. But when I noticed that after so much extremity I was still not seeing or loving You fully, I felt myself a failure.

My dear Lord Paramatma, I have been baptized so many times and have taken dozens of initiations. I have uttered hundreds of vows on so many altars, all for my cleansing and rectification. But after uttering all these words, finding that I still was not fully loving or seeing You, I felt myself a failure.

My dear Lord Paramatma, I have performed so many pious activities; I have fed the poor, housed the homeless and given clothes to the needy. On other occasions, I have advised the destitute, befriended the lonely and tried my hardest to protect the fearful. But through all this, as I noticed that I was not yet fully seeing or loving You, I felt myself to be a failure.

My dearest Lord Paramatma, I have wept myself to sleep many nights, believing that You had forsaken me. For long periods I have been obedient to every command that was given me. Yet instead of finding Your Lordship waiting at the end of the exercise, I have simply found emptiness and anxiety. I tried so many pathways in my search for You, but it was not until I realized that I was not yet eligible to receive what I was requesting that, from within my heart, You led me to a pure and qualified teacher.

This teacher heard my prayers and has now become very dear to me. You see, he has informed me that to reach You I cannot communicate through my hands, mouth, ears or eyes, but I must speak to You through my heart.

My loving teacher also informed me that until my heart could detect and distinguish You through the vision of selfless love and unconditional service, I would never see and love You fully. When my teacher finished instructing me, You personally supplemented his teachings and told me that, indeed, the heart language is most pure and sacred, but that it can only be learned through association with pure devotees.

Through Your causeless mercy, You revealed to me that the secret technologies for fully seeing and loving You are concealed within the bosoms of Your pure devotees. Then You further revealed to me that You in fact have only one secret hiding place: in the hearts of Your pure devotees. In the core of their hearts, You, the radiant Supersoul, reside in all of Your splendor.

My dear Lord Paramatma, now that I have made contact with the language of the heart through Your pure and loving representatives, I see and hear everything very differently.

Beloved Lord, I pray for the day that You will allow me to become fluent in this sacred heart language, so that I can one day be a carrier of Your essence. I long to love You fully and see You comfortably seated in my clean and devoted heart.

Chapter 18

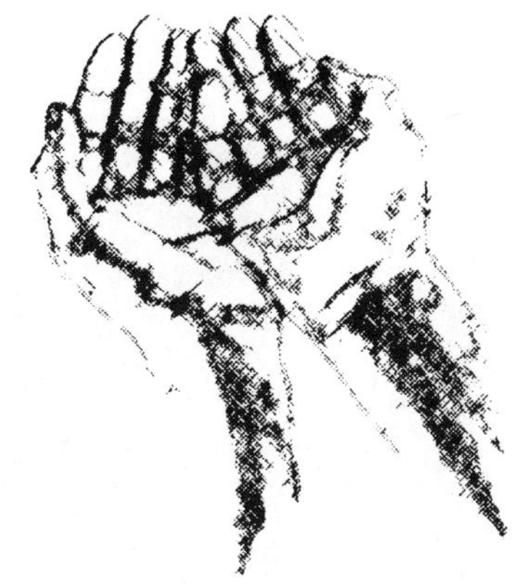

Showdown Of The Soul And Body

"Eventually the confusion got so intense that the Lord's agents almost gave up on me."
"That's when I again came along," my soul remarked, "and tried to intervene to redirect you. But this time, you attacked me with even greater vigor."

Recently my soul and body had a long-overdue confrontation, in celebration of their growth together. Feeling that my physical aspect had finally humbled and matured enough to hear a short account of its former faults, my soul playfully scolded its alter ego in a pleasant but provocative way.

"Remember those days when you were atheistic and wondered if there was actually a God?" My body silently winced to remember. "It took you quite a while, but when we finally reconciled that issue, you decided, 'Yes, God does exist, but He is the exclusive property of the Christians, Muslims and Buddhists—or anyone else who is following a bona fide tradition.'" My body's complexion reddened. "It seemed like it took an eternity before you realized that God literally has no favorites, and that He is never bribed by rituals or impressed by institutions."

Suddenly my body burst out laughing at itself. "If you think that's funny, remember how in the old days I used to totally identify with my economic status? There was one time when I actually believed that my tattered clothes were a permanent identity and that I was destined to be a pauper eternally.

"Hard as it is to fathom, it was only a few lifetimes later that I thought myself to be an elegant king." We both laughed loudly as my body lifted its shoulders and began strutting like a peacock. "And not just that, but I actually considered myself the owner of all that I surveyed. I had no inkling that since God owns and controls everything, I can never be poor or wealthy; I am simply the eternal servant of God and of His many servants."

"I remember that period, all right," my soul responded. "And that's not all I remember about it."

"You mean there's more?"

"Are you kidding? You used to be so proud of your mundane loyalty and industriousness that it was sickening. You prided yourself on being a dedicated, hardworking servant, and you thought yourself to be the greatest of *gurus* and teachers. You hadn't the faintest idea that all real knowledge and mastery are the automatic property of the soul."

Unable to defend itself, my body joined in the roast, finding new freedom in being able to laugh at itself. "Boy, was I silly," it laughed. "I mean, all those occasions when I thought I was a writer. What a joke! I can't say how many lifetimes it took me to realize that every single text I took credit for had been secretly whispered to me by the great unseen sages who not only had wisdom and experience far beyond my own, but were also generous enough to impart it internally to someone as unqualified as I was."

My soul heartily agreed and then added, "And just how many millennia did it take you to realize that all knowledge is contained in the Lord's Holy Name?"

"That's a good question. Actually; I'm not sure. I think I'm still working on that one. I'm still so caught up in my appearance. Sometimes it's as if I regress into a third-grader in a schoolyard; I get so uptight about being fat or skinny, tall or short, and I get so wrapped up in these temporary designations."

"The Sanskrit word for it is *upadi*," my soul replied cooly.

"You show-off! You're just lucky to be totally aloof from all activity and immune to mundane contamination. Still, you can't take any credit for your detachment; that's just your nature."

"That may be true, but I still can have a laugh at all those ridiculous changes you put us through in your efforts to survive and seek knowledge. I mean, let's face it. You used to be scared of everything! Rats, snakes, spiders, roaches. You would jump a mile just to dodge a tiny mosquito. There were times you were even scared of your own shadow."

My body tried to suppress a giggle, but could not contain itself.

"Yeah, that was pretty funny, but it was nothing compared to the challenge of breaking my bondage to lust. Everywhere I turned, something would attract me. I was like scrap metal being drawn to magnets, getting pulled toward temptations in every direction. It didn't matter whether I was in the waking, sleeping or dreaming state; I was utterly haunted by lust. The time of day didn't matter, nor did the part of the world, nor the season. Age, race or creed didn't matter. My tongue, my eyes, my ears—every part of me was subject to that slavery, and not one of my nine gates was immune to infiltration. But eventually, by the grace of God, I was able to curb that habit and transform my lust into love."

"Well, don't forget your false ego. It seems to me that your false ego was even more difficult to tame than your lust. I mean, even after you became immersed in religious activities, that ego of yours kept surfacing when we would least expect it."

My body painfully conceded. "I know. I hate to admit it, but so many times I performed the right action totally in the wrong consciousness. And any time I was commended for some activity, I would immediately try to claim credit for each success. I wanted everyone to notice how selfless, humble and spiritual I had become. It took me forever to realize that rather than acting like a saint, I should just be one."

"I guess you could have been one, if you hadn't been so busy whining about how lonely and abandoned you were, and how the mission was just too difficult for any one person to maintain."

"Well, it was."

"For one person, maybe it was. But you were never alone. You had thousands of helpmates. All around you, there were angels, sages, *devas, acharyas*—even the Supersoul came to your aid, not to mention the loving devotees. On both planes, people were constantly communicating with you and guiding you toward a full reconciliation with the Lord. But you were so pathetic. You were too busy listening to the mundane noise from the environment. You gave so much attention to your senses that you couldn't hear, see or feel the presence of either the Lord or His divine helpers."

Now my body hung its head in lamentation. "I know. I actually attacked a lot of those divine beings who came to rescue me. Although they were direct blessings from our worshipable Lord, I often saw them as my greatest enemies, while I considered my real enemies to be my friends.

Eventually the confusion got so intense that the Lord's agents almost gave up on me."

"That's when I again came along," my soul remarked, "and tried to intervene to redirect you. But this time, you attacked me with even greater vigor."

"The ironic thing is that all the while I was praying for guidance, clarity and intervention, but whenever it came along I would immediately attack the giver."

"That's when I personally started praying hard for you myself. Actually, we were about to give up on you altogether. I had packed it in, and was ready to take a long retreat. But just then, we noticed you beginning to relinquish your sense of proprietorship. And, strangely enough, just as you did this, you also began to drop a lot of your envy of the Supreme Lord. You even stopped categorizing everyone as friends and enemies, and pretty soon you weren't so distracted by happiness and distress. We were all kind of astonished." My soul paused. "But I remember that glorious day just as if it were yesterday."

Suddenly it was dead quiet. Neither of us spoke, but in a few moments my body approached my soul, shedding blissful tears of ecstasy. Although hardly able to compose itself, it beckoned for my soul to come forward, and when it did, my body spoke these words:

"My beloved essence: you have shown me Herculean patience and an abundance of unconditional love. You have been there for me when I was submerged in all kinds of illusions. You have rendered excellent care to my entire being and never ceased to soothe and comfort me. Please step forward and take full charge of all of our affairs from this day until forever."

At these words, my soul and body instantly embraced in union. Then my soul expanded and lovingly absorbed my physical aspect into its own eternal essence. From that point on, we two entities were merged into one integrated, absolute being, and we returned to the realm of our Eternal Father to continue frolicking in His eternal abode.

Chapter 19

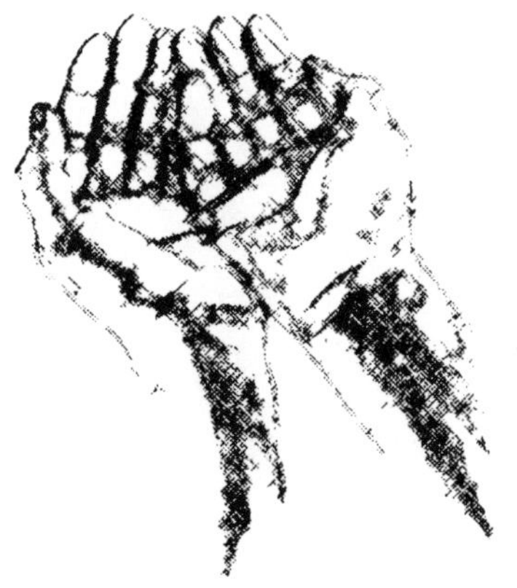

The Only Worthy Boon Is To Never Forget You

The Only Worthy Boon Is To Never Forget You 139

Dear Lord Krishna, when studying the lives of Your unalloyed devotees, one observes a most special characteristic. Whenever they are offered any boon, no matter how wonderful and alluring it may be, they never accept anything for their own sense gratification. The meditation of these great souls is always fixed at Your lotus feet. Is it any wonder that their only desire is to always serve You and never forget You?

The pseudo-devotee can easily be enticed by the glamour and comforts that *maya* offers. But Your unalloyed devotees get their full nourishment only by eating and drinking the sweetness of Your pastimes. In fact, Your *lila* is the pure devotees' luxury, their wealth and their very life air.

The materialists often have wonderfully attractive spouses who produce picture-perfect children. But to Your pure devotees, if such spouses are not on the path of *bhakti*, they are regarded as jackals and vampires who suck one's very life blood.

The materialists are also very expert in finding ways to prolong their health. They subscribe to elaborate health plans and insurance policies to cover all of their medical cares and expenses. What's more, these materialists go to spas and all kinds of elaborate facilities to exercise and stay in shape. Many of them exercise religiously, while others spend every dime they have pursuing treatments and cures for what are actually chronic diseases.

Bizarre as it seems, Your unalloyed devotees sometimes have the most wretched health, for they care little for their precious bodies and will gladly deny themselves in order to render service to others. Such devotees remain blissful even while enduring bodily ailments, because to them good health means nothing except as it relates to staying connected with You.

Materialists go mad searching for various decorations for their temporary material bodies. They keep abreast of every fad and invest in colorful, expensive clothing. They also wear and collect flashy jewelry just to attract the praise and attention of others. But Your unalloyed devotees have no interest in such nonsense. When they take pains to dress elegantly, their only concern is to dress for Your pleasure.

Materialists are always eager to attend banquets and parties where they can unwind and dance jubilantly. On such occasions they pump themselves full of intoxicants. But Your pure devotees are always dancing simply for Your pleasure, and for them this is the most satisfying intoxicant.

Materialists are also fond of all kinds of music. They buy records, tapes and CDs, and they all have their favorite recording artists. Your pure devotees are the greatest musicians, but they insist on only playing music that glorifies You and transports them into Your pastimes. O Govinda, Your pure devotees are especially attached to the sound of Your flute, which puts every atom of their bodies in ecstasy.

All materialists appreciate beautiful gardens, parks and well-built houses. Thinking themselves to be gods, they are always trying to establish kingdoms for their increased enjoyment. Your unalloyed devotees, however, simply see such places as elaborate prisons if Your glories are not sung there. When such beautiful parks and gardens are not utilized for Your glorification, Your pure devotees run as quickly from them as they would dash away from a poisonous snake.

Then there are Your mixed and partially covered devotees, who play the roles of naturalists and pseudo-religionists. Interested only in the superficial appearance of spirituality, these personalities spend billions of dollars to build gorgeous shrines in which to worship. They even visit these buildings regularly to pray, hear sermons and attend functions. But, unfortunately, even while ensconced in these holy shrines, they fail to summon Your holy presence by attracting You with real devotion.

Your pure devotees are not the least bit bewildered by all these false worshipers' mimicries of reverence. And because these places of worship are devoid of Your personal manifestation, presence and pastimes, Your unalloyed devotees consider them to be like cold dark pits or caves that lack light and proper amenities. Conversely, Your pure devotees consider places in which You are honestly glorified to be most sublime and venerable, regardless of how simple or imperfect they are.

If a place provides no glorification of Your Lordship and no association with Your devotees, then Your pure devotees consider such places to be most distasteful and unappealing. Even heaven feels hellish to such devotees without Your purifying presence. On the other hand, to Your pure devotees, even hellish worldly environments become Vaikuntha as soon as Your glories are sung there.

Dear merciful Lord, please allow me never to want or accept anything or any environment that is devoid of Your glorification. Help me to relish any environment where You dwell for even a moment, or where Your glories are genuinely sung. Most of all, help me to appreciate every soul who renders some service to You, no matter how crude or infinitesimal that service may seem to be.

O Lord, when will that day come that my heart will possess the sentiments of Your unalloyed pure devotees? I know that I am not worthy to enter into these ecstasies, but I can no longer bear to be bereft of them.

Purity is the force, but in me there is no purity to be found. So again, I beg you—please allow me to never forget You, because as Your pure devotees have demonstrated to us all, constant remembrance of You is the very passageway to unending pleasure. This is the only worthy boon.

Chapter 20

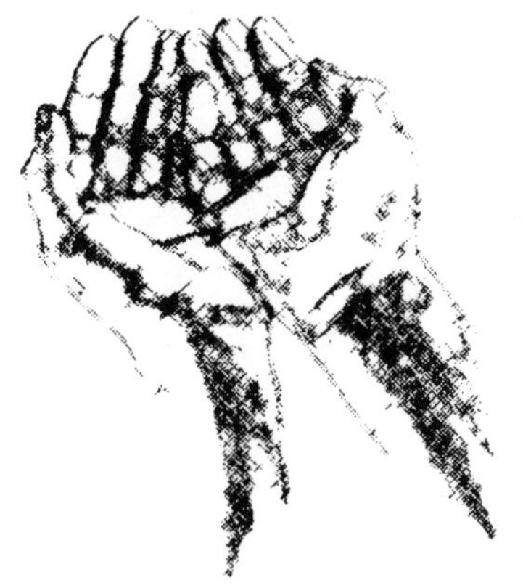

Spiritual Union vs. Material Sex Life

Dear soul within me, now that my gross and subtle physical aspects are finally becoming reacquainted with you, and we have begun to know and communicate with you, this conditioned self I call "me" has a few questions that only you can answer.

Here in the material world, everyone is intoxicated by sex life. Many people think about it constantly. Advertisers always capitalize on this addictive phenomenon and heartily feed our intoxication.

A person around someone of the opposite sex feels such a strong pull from the senses. Nowadays, many people are even stimulated by the same sex or both sexes. Some of the greatest art creations are expressions of subliminal and overt sexual urges. The basic goal of education, wealth, fame and prestige is simply to better facilitate one's sexual appetite and to find new sex partners.

My dear soul within me, nowadays adultery, prostitution and incest are common. In the near future all three may well be accepted as orthodox. Rape and even murder are on the increase daily, because people just can't control their agitation.

Leaders actually sacrifice their careers and empires, rather than withdraw from illicit sexual connections. Meanwhile, many of us, by simply seeing others engage in the sex act, become so stimulated and captivated that we totally lose all equilibrium. Even just hearing of another's sexual exploits can make us wild like maddened animals.

O soul within me, please let me know how these horrible disgraces have come about, so that I can better understand how I can free myself and others from this plague that is infecting everyone.

In the Age of Kali especially, we humans are a species controlled by the genitals. The genitals have become as central to us as our very brains, hearts and nervous systems. Everything is filtered through our sexual organs, and all of our thoughts, desires, concerns and aspirations must first consult with them and consider their gratification, stimulation and satisfaction before committing to anything.

Indeed, the physical "me" has come to understand why the apostle Paul taught Christians that, while it was best to be celibate like him, it would always be "better to marry than to burn."

The *Bhagavad-gita* explains that sex life is the shackle that binds us to the material world. The Song of God even says that when we ultimately give up sex life, fifty percent of our liberation is obtained. We also understand through the *Gita* that sex addiction is the main cause of our holding onto the bodily conception of life, and the reason we remain absorbed in temporary, trivial matters.

Suddenly, the soul within me spun a web of inner wisdom that clarified all of my confusion. "It is not sex life in and of itself that is evil. After all, in the *Bhagavad-gita*, Lord Sri Krishna explains to Arjuna that He Himself is sex life that is in accordance with religious principles. The problem is," my perfectly wise soul continued, "those who are on the bodily platform actually try to have union without union, and this is never possible. In the highest and most confidential aspects of all bona fide religious traditions, there are discussions of what constitutes real union—and this is always spiritual.

"One finds such sacred teachings in the Kabbalah, in Sufism, in the Book of Solomon, in the Bible, in bridal mysticism and throughout the *Bhagavat Purana* and its corollaries. In fact, the natural activity of the soul is either to be in constant union, or to be making arrangements for this dearly treasured and long-awaited divine union, which can only happen soul to soul. In the spiritual world, when union is thwarted or postponed, the living entity experiences the most exciting anticipation—a feeling that brings that entity closer than ever to God."

Then the spiritual "me," my soul, continued: "This material sex life, whose emblem is body consciousness, simply produces all kinds of socially disturbing consequences. Material sex life brings unwanted pregnancy and abortion, illegitimate children and venereal disease. Such unfortunate occurrences literally derail persons from the auspicious path of progress, and cheat innocent souls of many of the spiritual assets they have accrued. So listen well, my beloved, for although you are not yet ready to comprehend these transcendental affairs, one day soon this will all be commonplace to you."

I took in a breath, and tried to concentrate fully. "Union in the spiritual realm has nothing to do with physical bodies or genitals trying to find stimulation. You see, union between spiritual bodies in the spiritual world is not limited to genitals searching for contact. Rather, this sacred act involves all aspects of the spiritual body. All parts, layers and dimensions of the spiritual body engage in spiritual union, even when it is collective. In fact, in one's spiritual body, any sense can perform the activities of all the other senses. And, because spirit souls by their very nature are capable of far greater levels of harmony, when two souls unite for pleasure, other sincerely loving and empathetic souls who are fully tuned in to their frequency can also experience the union.

"In contrast to self-centered, lustful associations, these kinds of unions are inclusive rather than exclusive, because they are literally designed to cater to the common good and to fulfill the largest number of worthy persons."

As I tried to fathom this new reality, my inner self continued instructing me. "Material sex life and sex in the spiritual body are as different as oil and water, or as different as a sane and insane man. In the first case, although they are both liquids, they are completely incompatible. Similarly, although the sane and insane man are both men, their awareness is so totally different that while looking at the same surroundings, they each see completely different worlds.

"Another example is that of a noble, righteous citizen, who is free by dint of his upright character, versus a vicious, imprisoned criminal. Not only are these different kinds of men governed by different fields of activity, but in all three cases—the insane, the prisoners and those gripped by matter—the lifestyle and circumstances are perverted reflections of actual society. The environments of the prison and insane asylum are designed for chastisement and rehabilitation.

Worse still, when the prisoner forgets that he is incarcerated and continues sinning with other prisoners in an effort to enjoy his situation, he and all the others forfeit their parole.

"Likewise, conditioned souls who try to enjoy sex life outside of religious principles extend their periods of incarceration in the material sphere and prolong their subjugation to material afflictions."

At this point, my soul seemed to sigh, as if hoping I would not fall prey to such a fate. "As we converse more frequently, and as you continue to advance in spiritual life, you will give up the illusion of separateness. At that point, we shall finally reclaim our union and always relish divine association. When this happens, you will clearly understand how materialists are trying to have union without union, after which you will return to the spiritual world. There you will find everyone and everything in blissful union, constantly preparing for greater and more explosive encounters."

Chapter 21

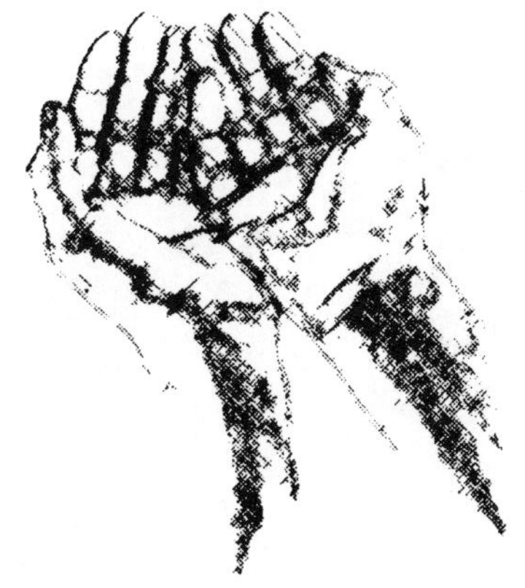

The Eternal Dance

"When the residents of the
spiritual world observe this
dance, they all collectively
enjoy the experience...Such is
the atmosphere of the eternal
dance that goes on daily in the
spiritual world."

My dear Lord Natabara, the most important days of our lives here in the material world are always celebrated with singing and dancing. It is a universal happening. On such occasions, we all put on our fanciest clothes and adorn ourselves with beautiful ornaments. But such activities are only reflections of the eternal dance that goes on daily in the spiritual world.

My dear Lord Natabara, in celebrating anniversaries, reunions, graduations, birthdays and weddings, we gather to sing and dance exuberantly. We even sometimes challenge and compete with one another in various playful ways. Shy ones become emboldened, and we all appreciate each other even more on these occasions.

On such occasions, there are few if any spectators, because everyone is enlivened, and all the musicians, dancers and singers have wonderful opportunities to express themselves. But such activities are only reflections of the eternal dance that goes on daily in the spiritual world.

My dear Lord Natabara, in the material world there are so many different dance styles: ballet, tap, folk, cultural, waltz, modern, slow and disco dancing. When the *gopis* and *gopas* dance for the Divine Couple, their dancing far surpasses all these styles. Their dances are faster, more colorful, more creative, extremely expressive and exquisitely graceful.

When one of the *gopis* or *gopas* dances, it is as if every *gopa* and *gopi* is dancing for Krishna's pleasure. When the residents of the spiritual world observe this dance, they all collectively enjoy the experience while they make their love offering to the Divine Couple. Such is the atmosphere of the eternal dance that goes on daily in the spiritual world.

My dear Lord Natabara, dance is the cultural and spiritual high point in many ethnic religious ceremonies, where the dancers must lose themselves to find themselves. As everyone jumps in to participate in the dance, each person momentarily forgets all problems and anxieties. Sometimes dancers are permanently able to resolve a dilemma by the inspiration or ecstasy that engulfs them, and thus they cancel out all inauspiciousness.

The Africans, Sufis, Jews, Eskimos, Native Americans and East Indians all have intense dance as a powerful cultural and religious expression. But such activities are only reflections of the eternal activities that go on daily in the spiritual world.

My dear Lord Natabara, when You and Your Divine Consort dance, all of the residents of the spiritual world drop everything to participate. The Divine Dance is the actual heart of the residents' activities; it is their very food and life air, and so each one pleads to have some involvement. There is no nourishment comparable to that of the dance.

In all the three worlds, there is no greater expression of expert dancing, no celebration more exhilarating, no fraternity more intimate and no exchanges more loving than those of the Divine Dance.

O, my dear Lord Natabara, when will that day come when I can also enter into this essence of all activities? One who doesn't participate in the Divine Dance is merely a member of the living dead. Therefore, my dear Lord, please allow me to rise from the living dead by giving me a glimpse of the Divine Dance, although I may never be qualified to participate.

Please, dear Lord Natabara, overlook my disqualifications and give me just one drop of the causeless mercy that You give even to the demons. I can never ask for more than this.

My dearest Lord Gauranga, You came to deliver the wretched, fallen souls by perfectly exhibiting the ecstatic dancing caused by *prema bhakti*. May I be carried by that wave of ecstasy and forget everything else.

Chapter 22

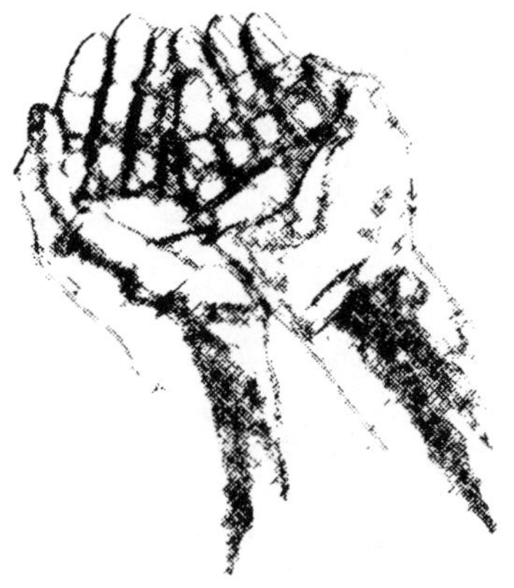

Divine Intimacy: First Contact With The Lord

"My dear
Lord Shyama,
when you first
make contact with
me, in what expression will it be?
...After You have made such intimate contact
with me, surely I will swoon in indescribable joy."

My dear Lord Shyama, will it be soon that I am able to gaze upon Your form of matchless beauty, and become totally enraptured? At that time my intelligence, mind and senses will all become one. They will no longer compete for selfish stimulation or domination, but will be in complete unison once and for all, eternally captured by their Divine Master.

My dear Lord Shyama, as I study Your exquisite, unparalleled beauty, I will feel ecstatic symptoms—weeping, quivering, stuttering and being stunned. Though I've waited so long and heard so much about them, these ecstatic symptoms will nevertheless surely hinder my vision of You, and my acute exhilaration will render me unconscious.

My dear Lord Shyama, as all of my senses withdraw from the sense of sight to the sense of smell, Your intoxicating fragrance will again cause me to lose consciousness. Each time I gain a bit of stability, I will find that all of my consciousness will totally align itself with one sense after another, just to be defeated again, unable to contain its tremendous joy and pleasure.

My dear Lord Shyama, when You first make contact with me, in what expression will it be? Will You place Your lotus feet on my head as You do to Your perfect servants who worship You in the mellow of servitorship?

Or will You entwine Your lotus fingers in mine as You do with those perfect servants who worship You in the mellow of friendship?

Maybe You will wipe away my tears with Your own lotus hands, as You do for those who worship You in the parental mellow. Or perhaps You will draw me to Your chest and wrap Your arms around me in a tender embrace, as You do for those amorous damsels who worship You in the conjugal mellow.

My dear Lord Shyama, after You have made such intimate contact with me, surely I will swoon in indescribable joy. That day, my happiness will know no bounds, as I will be able to relish all of Your transcendental qualities without hindrance. Wonderfully and magnanimously, this gift of supreme *prema* will install itself fully on the altar of my consciousness, and my heart will sing its jubilance.

My dearest Lord Shyama, at that time I will try to discover how this great fortune has come upon me. But the increasing bliss will not allow me even a moment to formulate my speech. Then, knowing my mind and heart, You will frankly answer my unformed question.

"My dear beloved," Lord Shyama addressed me, "for decades now, I have seen how crazy your mind was—how you were such a slave to your senses, and so totally full of doubts. I saw your persistent lack of gratitude and all of your ineptitude. You were swimming deep in the ocean of faults. But I also saw how much you desired to use everything that was yours in My service. I saw how you were hated, ridiculed and even attacked by envious personalities, and I saw that even though you were totally fearful, you did not once renounce My service even for a moment, nor did you even once deviate from your vows.

"Seeing your weak and helpless condition, but appreciating your determination, I therefore sent you a very special, first-class attendant from My abode—a guide to monitor, protect and eventually escort you directly to My residence.

"You were so crazy that you even doubted this special agent, and you gave him extreme difficulty. Except for his insistence that you weren't entirely hopeless, on several occasions I was prepared to call him back to Me, but each time I summoned him he assured Me that he would deliver you soon.

"My dear child, you remained determined to serve Me, but stubborn in so many areas. In fact, your every effort was far beneath the mark. Finally, to have the company of My loving agent once again, I decided to bestow causeless mercy on you, to receive you and make you worthy.

"You see, the intense selfless love between My unalloyed devotees and Me is something that even I have difficulty understanding. Because of this enigmatic love, I feel bound to deliver everyone whom these souls recommend to Me.

"Today you have experienced only a glimpse of what I have decided to make fully available to you, and already you can see what it has done to you. You have become renewed—and your heart has sung with untold jubilance."

Suddenly I felt embarrassed, remembering all my dullness, impatience and stubbornness. Tears flowed from my eyes, and my voice choked up as I tried to plead for forgiveness. But Lord Shyama simply turned toward me and showered me with loving glances. Then before I could respond, He unveiled for me a vision of His eternal abode, and I was utterly overwhelmed.

Finally, the Lord's sweet voice broke my *samadhi.* "My dear beloved, I am now your captive, fully under your control. Do not continue to be overwhelmed or disturbed. Just perceive Me and fulfill the desires of your heart. But for Me, no one can fully satisfy Your innermost longings. But fear not, for I am all yours and always have been. Now again, you, too, are all Mine as well... Welcome to eternity."

Glossary

Acharya: A spiritual teacher. One who teaches by example.

Bhagavad-gita: The "Song of the Supreme Lord." Sacred text of a conversation between Lord Krishna and His devotee Arjuna.

Bhajan: A song dedicated to the glories of the Lord.

Bhakta: A devotee of the Lord.

Bhakti: Spiritual love and devotion.

Bhakti yoga: Spiritual practices designed to lead the practitioner to love of God.

Brahmana, ksatriya, vaisya and **sudra:** The four divisions of society, according to the Vedic scriptures. The priestly class, kings and administrators, businesspeople and laborers, respectively.

Lord Brahma: Demigod commissioned to create and maintain the material universe under the Lord's direction. Considered the most advanced created living entity.

Lord Chaitanya Mahaprabhu: Incarnation of God who appeared as a humble devotee and showed by perfect example how to worship the Lord with love and devotion.

Heart chakra: One of several "centers" of the physical body (which include the head *chakra,* heart *chakra*, reproductive *chakra*, etc.). Love, compassion and devotion are anchored in the heart *chakra*.

Damodara: The Supreme Lord, appearing as a young, mischevious yet adorable child.

Devas: Angels and demigods.

Divine Couple: Mother-Father God. Known by name in the Vedic scriptures as Sri-Sri Radha-Krishna.

Gauranga: Another name for Lord Chaitanya Mahaprabhu, whose complexion resembled molten gold.

Gopinath: God as the eternal playmate and friend of the pure devotees.

Gopis and **gopas:** Eternal friends and playmates of the Lord.

Govinda: God as the giver of all pleasure and happiness.

Guru: A spiritual teacher. One who shows the way.

Gurukula: School system centered around teaching children the science of God-consciousness along with material skills.

ISKCON: The International Society for Krishna Consciousness. An international institution for spreading God-consciousness through out the world. It was founded by Swami Prabhupada.

Age of Kali: The age of quarrel and strife.

Kirtan: Songs glorifying the Lord and His eternal associates.

Krishna: God in His original form as the most attractive lover of all living entities.

Maya: The embodiment of illusion and darkness.

Natabara: The Lord in an eternally blissful, dancing incarnation.

Paramatma: The aspect of the Lord that resides within the heart of each living entity.

Prema bhakti: Loving devotional service to the Lord.

Samadhi: Trance or meditation.

Senapati bhakta: A great devotee who was predicted in the Vedic scriptures to travel the world spreading the message of love of God.

Supersoul: God as the original, supreme living entity guiding each of us from within. See Paramatma.

Shyama: God in a breathtakingly beautiful form, with a blackish complexion resembling a dark storm cloud.

Tirtha: Place of pilgrimage and refuge.

Vaikuntha: The eternal, spiritual residence of the Lord and His associates. Literally translates to "land of no anxieties."

Yamaraj: Demigod responsible for issuing rewards and punishment to the living entities according to their karma as they pass from one body to the next.

About The Author

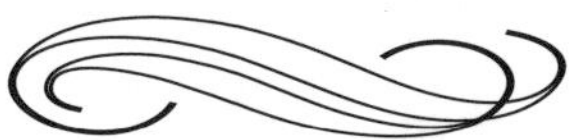

Bhakti-Tirtha Swami was born John E. Favors in a Christian, God-fearing family. As a child evangelist he appeared regularly on television. As a young man he was a leader in Dr. Martin Luther King's civil rights movement. At Princeton University he became president of the student council and also served as chairman of the Third World Coalition. Although his main degree is in psychology, he has received accolades in many other fields, including politics, African studies, Indology and international law.

His Holiness has served as Assistant Coordinator for penal reform programs in the State of New Jersey, Office of the Public Defender, and as a director of several drug abuse clinics in the United States. In addition, he has been a special consultant for Educational Testing Services in the U.S.A. and has managed campaigns for politicians. Bhakti-Tirtha Swami gained international recognition as a representative of the Bhaktivedanta Book Trust, particularly for his outstanding work with scholars in the formerly communist countries.

As the only African-American Vaishnava *guru* in the world, Bhakti-Tirtha Swami directly oversees projects in the United States (particularly Washington, D.C., Detroit and Pennsylvania), the Caribbean, West Africa and South Africa. He also serves as the director of the American Federation of Vaishnava Colleges and Schools.

In the United States, Bhakti-Tirtha Swami is the founder and director of the Institute for Applied Spiritual Technology, director of the International Committee for Urban Spiritual Development and one of the international coordinators of the Seventh Pan African Congress. Reflecting his wide range of interests, he is also a member of the Institute for Noetic Sciences, the Center for Defense Information, the United Nations Association for America, the National Peace Institute Foundation, the World Future Society and the Global Forum of Spiritual and Parliamentary Leaders.

A specialist in international relations and conflict resolution, Bhakti-Tirtha Swami constantly travels around the world and has become a spiritual consultant to many high-ranking members of the United Nations, to various celebrities and to several chiefs, kings and high court justices. In 1990 His Holiness was coronated as a high chief in Warri, Nigeria in recognition of his outstanding work in Africa and the world. In recent years, he has met several times with

President Mandela of South Africa to share visions and strategies for world peace.

In addition to encouraging self-sufficiency through the development of schools, clinics, farm projects and cottage industries, Bhakti-Tirtha Swami conducts seminars on spiritual development, interpersonal relationships, stress and time management and other pertinent topics. He is also widely acknowledged as a valuable participant in the resolution of global conflict.

The Beggar

Meditations and Prayers on the Supreme Lord

by Swami Krishnapada (B.T. Swami)

$11.95 softbound
160 pages, ISBN #1-885414-00-5

Serenity in the Lord

Deeply penetrating reflections in the form of a personal dialogue with God remind the reader of the necessity to dedicate time to spiritual growth along with secular pursuits. Written in an easily readable, non-sectarian style, this book explores such topics as patience, tolerance, humility, compassion and determination. The author presents these subjects not as quaint musings from another age but as necessary tools for maintaining sanity in a far-from-normal world full of conflict and stress.

"Now, my dear Lord, I am completely confused. I have tried to attract You, but I see I have nothing to attract You with. I am a pretender. I want Your kingdom, without You. I am a criminal who has tried to plead innocent, and now I have nowhere to hide, no presentations to make. What am I to do, dear Lord?

"Then I heard the Lord say: 'You have always been, and always will be, dear to Me, but you do not believe it. Therefore, you separate us by being an enemy to yourself. Come on, My child, and experience what it is to be fully dear to Me.'"

Excerpt from *The Beggar*

Available from your local bookseller, or just fill out the order form at the end of this book and fax it to the number below. You can also order by phone.
Telephone: (301) 261-4493 Fax: (301) 261-4797

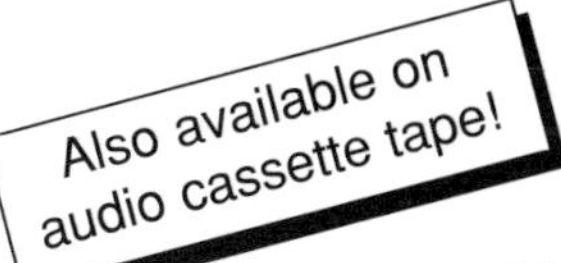

Spiritual Warrior II

Transforming Lust into Love

by Swami Krishnapada (B.T. Swami)

$20.00 hardbound, $12.95 softbound
248 pages

ISBN #1-885414-04-8 hardbound
ISBN #1-885414-03-X softbound

"*Spiritual Warrior II: Transforming Lust into Love* is a book to savor and treasure, a book that needs to be read and reread because of its spiritual potency and priceless value for everyday living....I am currently on my second and even third reading of certain chapters of this divinely inspired offering.... Everyone needs a copy of this book. "

Terry Cole-Whittaker. D.D.
Author of *What You Think of Me Is None of My Business*

Opening Your Heart

Today's world is suffering from an overdose of lust, while people everywhere are starving for love. In *Spiritual Warrior II*, Swami Krishnapada offers profound insight into the critical issues of the body, mind, and spirit that touch us all. Tough questions are addressed, such as: What is love? Where does lust come from? How can sexuality become a constructive force? How can we have better relationships? Provided with insightful answers stemming from a broad, compassionate, perspective deeply grounded in spirituality, we're shown how to live from the heart, loving ourselves, one another and God.

Available from your local bookseller, or just fill out the order form at the end of this book and fax it to the number below. You can also order by phone.
Telephone: (301) 261-4493 Fax: (301) 261-4797

Leadership for an Age of Higher Consciousness

Administration from a
Metaphysical Perspective

by Swami Krishnapada
(B.T. Swami)

$23.00 hardbound
$14.95 softbound
320 pages, ISBN #1-885414-02-1

"An example in the truest sense of global principle-centered leadership, Swami Krishnapada manages to take consciousness-raising to its highest platform of self-realized actuality in humanizing the work-place. My experience in working with all of the nations of the world convinces me that such a book is the corporate leadership guide for the coming millennium."

The Honorable Pierre Adossama
Director, Labor Relations (Retired)
International Labor Organization
United Nations

The Leader In You

Leadership in any capacity has taken on such awesome proportions that even the best leaders must find innovative and creative ways to deal with today's complex situations. *Leadership for an Age of Higher Consciousness: Administration from a Metaphysical Perspective* is a groundbreaking self-help manual written for those who seek to develop a more penetrating perspective and greater effectiveness in the leadership process. This book is relevant for heads of government, organizations and families, and for anyone seeking greater insight into self-leadership.

Available from your local bookseller, or just fill out the order form at the end of this book and fax it to the number below. You can also order by phone.
Telephone: (301) 261-4493 Fax: (301) 261-4797

by Swami Krishnapada
(B.T. Swami)

$12.95 softbound
200 pages, ISBN #1-885414-01-3

"As we rapidly approach the new millennium, more and more people are searching for spiritual answers to the meaning and purpose of life. The search, of course, begins with Self, and Swami Krishnapada's book, *Spiritual Warrior*, provides a practical companion for the journey of the initiate. I am honored to recommend it."

Gordon-Michael Scallion
Futurist; Editor,
Earth Changes Report
Matrix Institute, Inc.

Spiritual Warrior

Uncovering Spiritual Truths
in Psychic Phenomena

Ancient Mysteries Revealed!

Get ready for a roller-coaster ride into the intriguing realm of ancient mysteries! It is rare to find the subjects in this book handled in such a piercing and straightforward way. *Spiritual Warrior: Uncovering Spiritual Truths in Psychic Phenomena* focuses on the spiritual essence of many topics that have bewildered scholars and scientists for generations, such as extraterrestrials, the pyramids and psychic intrusion. A fresh perspective is revealed, inviting the reader to expand the boundaries of the mind and experience a true and lasting connection with the inner self.

Available from your local bookseller, or just fill out the order form at the end of this book and fax it to the number below. You can also order by phone.
Telephone: (301) 261-4493 Fax: (301) 261-4797

Order Form

HARI NAMA PRESS

☎ Telephone orders: 1-800-949-5333, (301) 261-4493

Fax orders: (301) 261-4797

✉ Postal orders: Hari-Nama Press
Capitol Hill, PO Box 76451, Washington DC 20013

▲ E-mail: ifast@com.bbt.se

● World Wide Web www.ifast.net/hnp

Please send the following: QTY

- **Leadership for an Age of Higher Consciousness**
  Hardbound $23.00 x ___ = $ ______
  Softbound $14.95 x ___ = $ ______
- **Spiritual Warrior: Uncovering Spiritual Truths in Psychic Phenomena** Softbound $12.95 x ___ = $ ______
- **Spiritual Warrior II: Transforming Lust into Love**
  Hardbound $20.00 x ___ = $ ______
  Softbound $12.95 x ___ = $ ______
- **The Beggar: Meditations and Prayers on the Supreme Lord** Softbound $11.95 x ___ = $ ______
- **The Beggar II: Crying Out for the Mercy**
  Softbound $11.95 x ___ = $ ______
- Yearly subscription to **Spiritual Warrior: The Quarterly Newsletter of the Institute for Applied Spiritual Technology** $10.00 x ___ = $ ______

Sales Tax: (MD residents add 5%) $ ______

S/H (see below) $ ______

TOTAL (Please make checks payable to Hari-Nama Press) $ ______

❍ I'd like more information on other books, audiotapes and videotapes from HNP.

Name: ____________________

Address: ____________________

City: ____________________ State: ________ Zip: ________

Daytime Phone: ________________ Evening Phone: ________________

Shipping and handling:

USA: $3.00 for first book and $1.75 for each additional book. Air mail per book (USA only): $4.00.
Outside of the USA: $8.00 for first book and $4.00 for each additional book.
Surface shipping may take 3-4 weeks. Foreign orders: please allow 6-8 weeks for delivery.